Harry Mengden Scarth

Aquæ Solis

Or Notices of Roman Bath

Harry Mengden Scarth

Aquæ Solis
Or Notices of Roman Bath

ISBN/EAN: 9783337270995

Printed in Europe, USA, Canada, Australia, Japan

Cover: Foto ©ninafisch / pixelio.de

More available books at **www.hansebooks.com**

AQUÆ SOLIS,

NOTICES OF ROMAN BATH;

BY

THE REV. H. M. SCARTH, M.A.,

PREBENDARY OF WELLS AND RECTOR OF BATHWICK;
MEMBER OF THE ARCHÆOLOGICAL INSTITUTE OF GREAT BRITAIN AND IRELAND; MEMBER OF THE BRITISH ARCHÆOLOGICAL
ASSOCIATION; MEMBER OF THE SOMERSET ARCHÆOLOGICAL AND NATURAL HISTORY SOCIETY, &c., &c., &c.

WITH FIFTY-TWO ILLUSTRATIONS BY C. S. BECKETT.

LONDON: SIMPKIN, MARSHALL, & CO., STATIONERS' HALL COURT.
BATH: R. E. PEACH, BRIDGE STREET.

1864.

"O that I had the Thracian Poet's harp
    For to awake out of th' infernal shade
Those antique Cæsars, sleeping long in dark,
    The which this ANCIENT CITY whilom made:
Or that I had Amphion's instrument,
    To quicken with his vital notes' accord,
The stony joints of these old walls now rent,
    By which the Ausonian light might be restored:
Or that at least I could with pencil fine
    Fashion the portraits of those palaces,
By pattern of great Virgil's spirit divine:
    I would assay with that which in me is,
      To build with level of my humble style
      That which no hands can ever more compile."
                      —SPENSER.

TO THE

LORD TALBOT DE MALAHIDE,

F.S.A., M.R.I.A., &c., &c.,

VICE PRESIDENT OF THE ARCHÆOLOGICAL INSTITUTE

OF GREAT BRITAIN AND IRELAND,

THIS VOLUME

IS (WITH HIS LORDSHIP'S PERMISSION)

DEDICATED, WITH EVERY SENTIMENT OF DEEP RESPECT,

BY THE AUTHOR.

INTRODUCTION.

MANY writers of later times have treated of the Antiquities of BATH; the fragments of Sculpture and Inscribed Stones discovered at different periods having caused considerable attention to be given to the subject. LELAND[1] recounts what he saw in the City Walls when he made his journey through the Western part of England in the reign of HENRY VIII., and CAMDEN[2], in his Britannia (Somerset), devotes much space to the mention of the Roman Remains at BATH.

HORSLEY[2] has furnished a list of what had been collected in his day. The late Rev. THOMAS LEMAN, Chancellor of Cloyne, who spent much of the latter portion of his life in BATH, and devoted himself to the study of the Roman Remains, in his annotated copy of HORSLEY'S B. R., which he bequeathed to the Literary and Scientific Institution in the city, has given many valuable notes in his own handwriting. Dr. GUIDOTT[3] treats of the Roman Antiquities of BATH, and gives drawings of Sculptures at his time existing in the Walls; he also records some Inscriptions and Coins, but unhappily the Inscriptions are all lost, and his published drawings are of doubtful accuracy.

Dr. MUSGRAVE[4] treats of the Roman Antiquities of BATH; and Dr. LUCAS and Dr. SUTHERLAND[5] record the discoveries made in their days.

[1] Itinerary, vol. ii., second edition; Oxford, 1744.
[2] Britan. Rom., published 1732, p. 323 et seq.
[3] Discourse of Bathe, and the Hot Waters there, published A.D. 1676, ch. x.
[4] Bel: Brit: 2 vols., Exeter.
[5] See Attempt to Revive Ancient Medical Doctrines; London, 1763.

vi.

In more recent times, the Rev. RICHARD WARNER published his Illustrations of the Roman Antiquities discovered at BATH, A.D. 1797: the work was under the patronage of the Mayor and Corporation of the City, to whom it was dedicated. He collected together records of all that had been discovered up to his time, and prefaced his account with an introduction, treating of the probable date of the foundation of the Roman City. This is also done in his History of BATH.[1] His plates, however, are coarse; in many cases his readings of the Inscriptions are incorrect; and his descriptions, although accompanied with many classical quotations and historical allusions, are not always accurate.

The beautiful work of Mr. LYSONS, forming the second part of his Reliquiæ Romanæ, is a noble contribution to Archæology, and has done ample justice to the Remains found in BATH, but since the date of the publication of that work, new discoveries have been made, and the progress of Archæology has thrown fresh light upon the readings of Inscriptions which were then doubtful. CARTER's plates have also faithfully delineated many of the Roman Remains. POWNALL and WOOD have added the results of their researches.

The Historians of the County of Somerset have entered very fully into the Roman Antiquities. The Rev. JOHN COLLINSON, F.S.A., in his History of Somerset,[2] and the Rev. W. PHELPS,[3] devote ample attention to the subject, and give many illustrations. Some Papers have appeared in the Archæologia in past years,[4] and latterly an able Paper by Mr. SCHARF, on the Pediment of the Temple of Minerva.[5] The Somerset Archæological and Natural History Society have also published Papers on the Roman Antiquities of Bath, in their Annual Volumes; and the Journal of the British Archæological Association contains the groundwork of the present work, in the series of Papers on the Roman Antiquities of BATH which have appeared in that publication.

The late Mr. HUNTER, one of the assistant keepers of the Public Records, while resident in BATH, devoted much time to forming a complete Catalogue of the Roman Antiquities of BATH, in which he was assisted by Mr. LONSDALE.

[1] See ch. ii., published A.D. 1801.
[2] Vol. i., p. 7, and following.
[3] Vol. i., p. 154, and following.
[4] See Vol. x., p. 325, xxii., p. 420, Appendix.
[5] See Vol. xxxvi., p. 187.

The Remains which were first collected together in a Museum in Bath Street were afterwards transferred to the Literary and Scientific Institution, and deposited there by the Corporation when the Literary Institution was opened, in 1825.[1] The arrangement of the Antiquities and the formation of the MS. Catalogue was chiefly owing to the labours of Mr. HUNTER, who executed the work with much care and considerable learning, and had the advantage of the works on BATH Roman Antiquities previously published to aid him. To this I have been chiefly indebted for information on the Roman Antiquities of BATH, but it is hoped that the present volume may rectify some mistakes occurring in the reading of the Inscriptions, while it also contains some new Inscriptions which have been found since the date of Mr. HUNTER's Catalogue. It was at first intended simply to publish an Illustrated Catalogue of the Roman Remains in BATH, like those which are to be found in some of our provincial cities, but the subject when once entered upon grew in importance, and induced the attempt at a volume similar in design to Mr. ROACH SMITH's Roman London. The careful Anastatic drawings also of an amateur artist, who most kindly and ably co-operated in the work, have led to the hope that a more extended account may not prove unacceptable to the public.

The author's great object has been to collect together into one volume every fragment of the Roman times which is known to have existed or is still preserved, and thus to help forward an accurate knowledge of the condition of the City while under Roman occupation. Great care has been bestowed upon the Inscriptions, which are full of interest to the Archæological student, and the architectural details have been given with as much fidelity as possible. Truth and accuracy have been sought after rather than theory or conjecture, and the records of past ages have been consulted rather than any new opinions propounded. It is the duty of the student of antiquity to collate and compare rather than hastily to assert, and if in the descriptions of the Roman Remains of BATH any errors should be found, it is hoped that they may be attributed to pressure of engagements rather than neglect of research. The following work is the result of leisure hours occupied in the study of antiquities as a relaxation from more serious duties, and undertaken solely from a desire to preserve, and to render accessible to all, a knowledge

[1] See Connection of Bath with the Literature and Science of England, a Paper read before the Literary and Philosophical Association, by the Rev. JOSEPH HUNTER, F.S.A., p. 119; Reprinted and Published by R. E. PEACH, Bath, 1853.

of those monuments of antiquity which yet remain, and an examination of which will tend greatly to encourage and enliven, as well as to assist, the study of history.

If any one will compare BATH as it is, with BATH as it existed in the Roman period, he will in some degree realise the changes that have passed over the City in the lapse of fifteen or sixteen centuries; and if he would understand the growth and developement of society, and the blessings which Christianity has brought with it, he cannot have a more profitable study than that of ancient remains. The study is not a dry collation of meaningless relics, but the gathering together of speaking memorials, which tell indeed of luxury, pomp, and display, but of superstition and ignorance, and that hopeless condition in which Heathenism had involved mankind.

The natural features of the country remain unchanged, the Springs pour forth their healing as they did of old, but a free, active, enlightened, united, and strong people, governed by just laws, and encouraged to active endeavours, have taken the place of an enslaved and degenerate race, the victims of oppression and cruelty. If we view the Roman dominion under its most favourable aspect, as the civilizer as well as the subjugator of the people brought within its grasp,—if we regard it as the means of humanising and refining a people, and preparing the way for better knowledge, we can yet find deep traces of ignorance and barbarism, from which we are wholly emancipated, and which may well kindle within ourselves unbounded gratitude. The Roman occupation of this Island must ever have a peculiar interest for its inhabitants, when the effect it has had upon our language and laws is considered. Much more is due to the Roman dominion than is generally supposed, and it is only by studying the remains of art, the inscriptions, and the language of that people, that we can adequately estimate the effect of their rule. To collect together, therefore, and arrange such memorials as still exist can never be an unprofitable labour.

In conclusion, the Author of the present volume ought to express his thanks to those who have so readily aided him in the work, especially to the Lady by whom all the Illustrations have been drawn; to Mr. JOSIAH GOODWIN, F.S.A., for assistance: and to Mr. EZRA HUNT and others, for local information received from them.

INDEX TO THE PLATES.

FRONTISPIECE—Bronze Head found in Bath.

PLATE I. Sculptures once in the Walls of Bath, restored from drawings given by Guidott — opposite page 11
" II. Corinthian Column ... ... opp. p. 15
" III. Pediment of Temple, and Inscription supposed to belong to it ... ... opp. p. 18
" IV. Fragments found under the Pump Room, opp. p. 22
" V. Fragments of Sculptures of the Seasons, opp. p. 23
" VI. Head of Luna, with Fragments and Inscription found with it ... ... opp. p. 24
" VII. Roman Female Head found in Bath, now walled into the Porch of a House in Musgrave's Alley, Exeter ... ... opp. p. 27
" VIII. Roman Pig of Lead ... ... opp. p. 28
" IX. Medicine Stamp, and Sculpture of a Dog carrying a Deer, found in Bath on the line of the Fosse Road ... ... opp. p. 32
" X. Altar to Jupiter and Hercules Bibax ... opp. p. 40
" XI. Altar in the Bestrees of the Parish Church of Compton Dando, with the figures of Hercules and Apollo ... ... opp. p. 41
" XII. Altar to the Loucetian Mars and Nemetona, ... opp. p. 42
" XIII. Altar erected to the Goddess Sul Minerva, by Sulinus, the son of Maturus ... opp. p. 47
" XIV. Altar to Sul Minerva et numine Augustorum, erected by Curiatius Saturninus ... opp. p. 48
" XV. Altar erected to the goddess Sul by Marcus Aufidius Lemnus, for the health and safety of Aufidius Maximus ... ... opp. p. 49
" XVI. Altar dedicated to the goddess Sul for the health and safety of Aufidius Maximus, by his freedman Aufidius Eutuches ... opp. p. 50
" XVII. Altar to the Suleves, erected by Sulinus the carver ... ... opp. p. 52
" XVIII. Funereal Stone to Calpurnius Receptus, priest of the goddess Sul ... ... opp. p. 54
" XIX. Funereal Stone to Rusonia Aventina ... opp. p. 56
" XX. Funereal Stone to a soldier of the Twentieth Legion ... ... opp. p. 58
" XXI. Funereal Stone erected to Julius Vitalis, opp. p. 59
" XXII. Funereal Stones found at Bath, but now lost ... ... opp. p. 62
" XXIII. Portions of two Stones erected to Roman Cavalry, the lower being that of Tancinus, a Spaniard ... ... opp. p. 64
" XXIV. Altar erected by Vettius Benignus ... opp. p. 66

PLATE XXV. Altar erected to commemorate the restoration of a "Locus Religiosus" ... ... opp. p. 68
" XXVI. Funereal Stone to Succia Petronia ... opp. p. 70
" XXVII. Funereal Stone to an Alemannus ... opp. p. 72
" XXVIII. Part of an Inscription put up by Novantius in consequence of a dream ... ... opp. p. 73
" XXIX. Inscription found at Combe Down, having been used as a covering Stone to a Coffin of the same material ... ... opp. p. 74
" XXX. Fragment of a Marble Tablet, and fragment of an Inscription on Sandstone ... opp. p. 77
" XXXI. Stone found in Bath ... ... opp. p. 81
" XXXII. Stone found in Bath ... ... opp. p. 82
" XXXIII. Roman Fragments found in Bath, opp. p. 83
" XXXIV. Locket found in Bath, under the Pump Room ... ... opp. p. 84
" XXXV. Patatae, Roman Keys, and Fibula, opp. p. 85
" XXXVI. A. Roman Flue-tile, semicircular; B. Floor-tile, with opening on the side; C. Flue-tile, wedge shaped, with circular holes as if to admit a pipe; D. pattern of Roman tessellated Pavement found under the new building of the Mineral Water Hospital; E. pattern of Pavement found under the Bluecoat School ... ... opp. p. 88
" XXXVII. Small Roman Vase of Black Ware, found in the Sydney Gardens, A.D. 1828 ... opp. p. 91
" XXXVIII. Roman Urn, found in Bath (Red Ware), ... opp. p. 92
" XXXIX. Samian Bowls, restored from Fragments found in Bath ... ... opp. p. 93
" XL. Roman Bowls and Samian Ware, restored from Fragments found in Bath ... ... opp. p. 94
" XLI. Fragments of Samian Ware found in Bath, opp. p. —
" XLII. Samian Ware, and patterns enlarged, opp. p. —
" XLIII. Samian Ware found in Bath ... opp. p. —
" XLIV. Roman Glass Vessels found at Combe Down, A.D. 1881 (actual size) ... ... opp. p. 90
" XLV. Roman Ampulla of Glass, found in a Stone Coffin at Swainswick, near Bath, A.D. 1840, opp. p. 98
" XLVI. Fragment of Sculpture found at Wellow, opp. p. 114
" XLVII. Tessellated Pavement found at Newton-St.-Loe ... ... opp. p. 115
" XLVIII. } Cups found on the site of a Roman Villa,
" XLIX. } Combe Down ... ... opp. p. 117
" L. Bronze Articles found on the site of a Roman Villa, Combe Down ... ... opp. p. 118
" LI. Capital of Column found near Warleigh, opp. p. 119

PLANS.

1. The old Roman Baths.
2. Roman Roads, Camps, Villas, and Earthworks within a Circuit of Seven Miles of BATH.

TABLE OF CONTENTS.

	Page.
INTRODUCTION	
ROMAN OCCUPATION OF BATH ; NAME AND ORIGIN OF AQUÆ SOLIS	1
THE ANCIENT ROMAN WALLS	7
THE FORUM	12
ANCIENT ROMAN BATHS	14
PLAN OF DITTO	14
REMAINS OF THE TEMPLE OF MINERVA	17
BRONZE HEAD OF PALLAS (VIDE FRONTISPIECE)	26
ROMAN METALLURGY	29
ROMAN MEDICINE STAMP	32
SCULPTURE OF A DOG CARRYING A DEER	34
GRANT OF ROMAN CITIZENSHIP FOUND IN BATH	36
ROMAN ALTARS AND INSCRIPTIONS	38
FUNEREAL INSCRIPTIONS	50
SCULPTURED STONES	51
ROMAN FRAGMENTS	53
BRONZE MEDALLION	54
PENATES	55
CONSTRUCTION OF HYPOCAUSTS AND TESSELLATED FLOORS	58
TESSELLATED PAVEMENTS FOUND IN BATH	59
ROMAN POTTERY, TILES, AND GLASS	81 83 91
ROMAN INTERMENTS	97
ROMAN ROADS	106
MAP OF AQUÆ SOLIS AND ITS ENVIRONS	106
VESTIGES OF ROMAN VILLAS IN THE VICINITY OF AQUÆ SOLIS	111
ROMAN CAMPS AND EARTHWORKS	129
ROMAN COINS FOUND IN BATH AND THE NEIGHBOURHOOD	131
ROMAN REMAINS RECENTLY DISCOVERED IN BATH	136
LIST OF SUBSCRIBERS	134

INDEX.

A.

	PAGE
Abbey Church, Bath	12 13
Abbey Church Yard	13
Agricola	16 20
Alumnus	...
Andraste or Andate	72
Antijacobin Review	45 46
Antinous, Statue of	2
Antoninus Itinerary of	2 3 4 108
Antoninus Pius, Coin of	136
Apollo, controversy about head of	20
Aquæ Calidæ	1
Artis's Durobrivæ	3
Ash Farm, North Stoke, Roman Villa	130
Astarte	45
Aubrey, John, Antiquary, account of Tessellated Floor found at Bathford	119 120
Aufidius Maximus	49 50 51
Aufidius Eutuches	50
Augustine, Saint	4
Aulus Plautius	5
Avon	1

B.

Baal, Worship of	45 46
Banner Down	119
Barratt, Mr. Joseph	36
Bath, a Roman, discovered at Bitton	125 130
Baths, Ancient Roman	14
Beach Farm, Roman Villa	119
Belgæ	5
Belga (Nations)	50
Bertram, his Tres Scriptores	102
Berwick Camp	128
Bettington, J., Esq.	131
Bignor, Roman Villa	147
Birch, Anc. Rom. pottery	55
Bitton	130
Blagdon, Blackdown Range, Mendip Hills	4 29
Blue Coat School, Tessellated Pavement found under Borough Walls Camp	1 128
Box, Roman Villa	119
Brean Down	30
Bristol	136
Britton, Antiquary	12 22
Brugniart Mons.	23
Bronze Medallion	54
Buckman, Professor	12
Burnett, Corston Parish, Roman Villa	126
Tessellated Pavement	127
Burton's Commentary on Antonine	74

C.

	PAGE
Caerleon	5 24 53 108 109
Caerwent	108 109
Cæsar	20 44
Calpurnius, C., Funeral Monument	51 55
Calpurnius Agricola	54 55
Calpurnus	55
Camden, Historian	7 10 11 12
Camden, B. R.—Introduction	v.
Camerton, Inscription found at	72
Camerton, Roman Remains	128
Campo Vaccino, Rome	15
Camps, Roman, around Bath	124 125
Carter, Mr.	22
Carter, his Plates—Introduction	vi.
Caurisvis	64
Ceawlin, Saxon King	6
Charlecombe, Interment discovered near	105
Charterhouse on Mendip	30
Chester	5 17 18 19
Cheyney Court, Roman Villa	119
Child, Mr. Francis	27
Cirencester (Anc. Corinium)	13
Cist, Stone, found at Lockerbrook	104
Civis Mediomatrica	57
Civis Trever	57
Civis Hispanus	64
Civium Romanorum	64
Claudian	...
Claudius, Emperor	4 5
Clifton, Camp opposite	128
Coffin, Leaden, found near Sydney Buildings	29 111
Coffin Tining, Lansdown	125
Coin of Augustus	131 132
Coins, Roman, Collections of	131 132 133
Coins, Roman, found in Bath	25
" " found under new portion of Mineral Water Hospital	30 124
" " found in Walcot	30
" " found near the East Gate	29
" " found on the site of Sydney Buildings	29
" " found in Cemetery, Lyncombe	112
" " found in Cemetery, Bathwick	...
" " Silver, found near Sydney Buildings	110
" " found at Bitton	135
" " found at Combe Down	134
Colerne, Roman Villa near	120
Collinson, Hist. of Somersetshire	vi. 8 11
Colossal Female Head of Stone	27
Collegium	59
Colonia Glev.	63

INDEX.

	PAGE
Column, Roman Capital, found near Bathford	119
Combe Down	5
Combe Down, Inscription found at	75
Combe Down, Roman Villa	116
" List of Roman and other remains	117, 118
Compton Dando, Altar in Buttress of Church	41, 46
Congrove, Roman Villa	120
Cornelianus, Inscription	78
Corinthian Capital	19, 14
Crunch, Mr. John	26, 119
Cruickshank, Mr.	134

D.

Dumnonii	41
Decurio	62, 63
Dscurienes	63
Dion Cassius, Historian	4
Dogs, Roman and British, in Sculpture and on pottery	35
Domitian, Emperor	22
Dundry Hill	1
Dyrham, Battle of	6

E.

Earthworks around Bath	128, 129
Edward the Confessor, Laws of	146
Ellacombe, Rev. H. T.	134
Englefield, Sir H., gives a cast of Bronze Head found in Bath to Soc. of Antiq.	85
Ex Viso	73

F.

Fabrica	58
Fabricienais	60
Farley Castle, Roman Villa near	121
Farmer's Field, near Tracy Park, Roman Villa	125
Forum, Anc. Rom.	9, 12
Foss Road	8, 20, 106, 107
Fragments, Roman, found in Bath	63
Funereal Inscriptions	60

G.

Gaius Tiberinus, Stone erected by	58
Gale, Antiquary	102
Gates of Roman Bath	2
Geoffrey of Monmouth	2
Glass, Roman	95
Glevum	63
Godwin, Mr. E. W., account of Roman Villa at Colerne	121
Goodridge, Mr.	113
Gough, Mr., observations on Stamps and Seals	34
Grants of Roman Citizenship	36, 37
Guest, Dr.	106, 107
Grenville, Sir Beville's Monument	129
Guidott, Dr.—Introduction v. 10, 11, 13, 20, 74, 133

H.

Hadrian, Emperor	4, 27, 29, 32
Hampton Down	16, 124
Hanham Green, Roman Villa	125
Hartshorne, Salopia Antiqua	44
Hasilbury, Roman Villa	120

	PAGE
Hearne, Antiquary	111
Heathcote Rev. G.	121
Henry VIII, King	10
Hispanus	64
Hoare, Sir R. C.	1, 2, b, 44
Hoare, Mr.	44
Homer	21
Horsley	v. 71
Hunter, Mr.	vi. 2, 63, 72
Hypocaust, described	64

I.

Iford, Roman Villa	121
Inscription, Runic	144
Interments, Roman	47
Iter XI., of Richard of Cirencester	106
Iter XIV., of Antoninus	145

J.

Julius Vitalis, Stone erected to	52
Juvenal, Satirist	57

K.

Keys Roman	71
Kingston Baths	13

L.

Lancaster	21
Langridge, Roman Villa	121
Lanedown, Roman Villas	120
Lansdown, Camps on	127
Latinus, M. Valerius, Stone erected to	64
Laws of the Twelve Tables	115
Lead Mines, Roman	4, 24
Lee, Mr.	24, 26
Leemans, Dr. Conrad	65
Legio Secunda, AD., P. F.	61
Legio XIII., Gem.	34
Leithieullier, Mr.	34
Leland, Antiquary	v. 7, 9, 10, 11, 51
Leman, Rev. Thos.	v. 3, 11, 107, 121
Lemnus, Marcus Aufidius, Altar erected by, to the Goddess Sul	4
Lilley, Mr., Bookseller	20
Lion of Stone found	132
Locus Religiosus	68
Lonsdale Mr.	vi.
Lucas, Dr.	v. 13, 14, 15
Lucian	114
Luxborough, near Dunster, Mining Implements found	31
Lydney, Roman Villa	127
Lysons	vi. 2, 14, 19, 24, 27, 36
Lysons, Rev. S.	29

M.

Maesbury Camp	30
Macekool	134
Maison Carrée, at Nismes	30
Marble, fragment of Inscription on	44
Market, New	127
Mars, Altar to, found at Brigual, near Greta Bridge, Yorkshire	41

INDEX.   xii

	PAGE
Mars, Loucetius	42 43
Martel de Fer, found in Stone Coffin, Langridge	125
Masters, Miss	18
McCaul, Dr. 20 21 32 23 34 27 43 54 55 56 62 64 70	
Medicine Stamp ... 32 23 24	
Mediomatrices Civea ... 46	
Mediomatrici, a people of Gaul ... 46	
Mendip Hills ... 46	
Metallurgy, Roman ... 82	
Minerva, Ægis of ... 12	
Minerva, Goddess 12 13 21	
Minerva, Bronze Head of ... 25	
Mines, Mendip ... 29	
Modestius, C. Murrius, Stone erected to ... 61	
Monks' Mill, Bath ... 5	
Musgrave, Dr. v. 1 2 27 28 26 27	
Museum of Bath Antiquities first formed ... 25	
Museum at Taunton ... 30	

N.

Nemetona, Altar to	42 43
Newmarch, C. H., Esq., Illustrations of Rom. Art in Cirencester	19
Newton St. Loe, Roman Villa	114 115
Nichols, Rev. W. L., his "Horæ Romanæ"	114 115
Nicomedia	65
Novanti Filius	73
Numina Augustorum	45

O.

Oppian	35
Optiones	84
Ormerod Mr.	102 109 110

P.

Pallas or Minerva, Bronze Head of	25
Pallas Athene	45
Park, Victoria, Interments discovered in	110
Pembroke, Lord	28
Penates	45
Phelps, Rev. W., History of Somersetshire—Intro. vi	29
Pigot, Mr., possessed Cast of Head said to have been found in Bath	25
Pig of Lead, Roman, found on site of Sydney Buildings	29
Pinnacle of Villa found at Wellow	113
Philipos	74
Pliny	27
Pompeii, Medallion of	24
Potters' Kilns, Roman	23
Potters' Stamps	25
Pottery, Roman, found in Sydney Gardens	91
" found in Walcot	91
Pottery, Roman, list of, found under new portion of Mineral Water Hospital	91
" found near the East Gate	102
" in Russell Street	103
Pownall, Governor vi. 1 2 12 20 21	
Præfecti	63
Principia	75 76
Prior Park	12b
Proclus, a late Greek writer	83

	PAGE
Ptolemy, geographer	1 2
Pump Room, Bath	12 13 17 18

R.

Ravenna List	2
Rectory, Bathwick	137
Remains, Roman, recently found	136 137
Ribchester	22
Richard's Itinerary	2 3 4 61
Richard of Cirencester	101
Rosin, Roman	1
Ruber Codex, or Red Book of Bath	1
Rusmia Avenus, Monument to	66

S.

Sacratissima (Epithet)	26 27
Sainsbury, Messrs.	137
Salisbury Plain	4
Salisbury Camp	12a
Salisbury Hill	4
Salisbury Crags	4
Samian Ware, manufacture of	91 92
Saturninus, C. Curistius, Altar erected by	42
Saxon Monastery, Bath	18
Saxon Regal Palace	18
Scharf Mr.	17 21 22 23 24
Schweighauser, M.	46
Scrope, Powlett, Esq., M.P., description of Roman Villa, North Wraxall	123
Sculpture of a Dog carrying a Deer	33
Sculptured Stones found in Bath	21
Secundus, Julius (Century of)	61
Sextius, L. Ulpius	56
Severn, River	4
Severius, C. Emeritus	64
Sydney Buildings, Bath	
Signifer	83
Silbury Hill	4
Simpson, Dr., of Edinburgh	31
Skeleton, found at the Gas Works	32
" in Bathwick Cemetery	137
" in Villa Fields	101
" in Lockbrook	103
Skinner, Rev. J.	82
Shrine, H. D., Esq., Roman Villa on his property near Warleigh	119
Smith Mr. Leach	17 43 78
Solinus	2 4 13 82
Solsbury Hill	4
Spry, Dr.	15 26
St. John's Church, Bathwick, Roman Remains found	137
St. Michael	45
St. Michael's Church	45
Stalls Church	12 45
Stantonbury Camp	12a
Stone Coffins found	30
Stone Coffins	97
" found at St. Catherine's Hermitage	
" on the premises of Messrs. Sainsbury, Walcot	119
" in the Orange Grove	26
" opposite No. 15, Russell Street	92 103

INDEX.

	PAGE
Stone Coffins found near Burnt-House Turnpike Gate	99
„ at Lambridge	99
„ on foundation of St. Stephen's Church	99
„ near Sydney Buildings	90 100 101
„ in Sydney Gardens	101
„ in Lyncombe Vale	102
„ Weston Farm House	103
„ Lockebrook	103
„ Langridge	104
Strabo	35
Strator Consularis	57
Stukeley, Dr.	7 13 71
Successa Petronia (Inscription to)	70
Sudbrook Camp	109
Suetonius, Historian	5
Sul	25 44 45 49 50 53 54 55
Sulinus, Son of Maturus, Altar erected by	47
Sulinus, Sculptor	52
Sul—Minerva	22 24 44 47 48
Sulova	52
Sutherland Dr.	v. 13 15

T.

	PAGE
Tabula Honestæ Missionis	36 37
Tacitus, Historian	5 16
Tancinus, L. Vitellius, Stone erected to	64 65
Temple, Roman	12
„ of Minerva	17
„ of Jupiter Stator at Rome	18
„ Inscription on Pediment	19 20 21
„ Tympanum of Pediment	21
Tessellated Floors	67 88
„ „ found under new portion of Mineral Water Hospital	89
„ „ under Blue Coat School	89
Tessellated Pavements in the Abbey Green	89
„ „ corner of Bridewell Lane	90
„ „ on the site of ancient Roman Baths	90
„ „ in Walcot	90
Tessellated Pavement found at Wellow	113
„ „ near Newton St. Loe	114
Tiles, Roman	96
Titus	5
Tite, W., Esq., M.P.	17 18
Thames, River	5
Tombelaine, Mount, near Avranches, France	45

U. V.

	PAGE
Trajan, Emperor	36 37
Trajectus	109
United Hospital Albert Wing	126 127
Uriconium (Wroxeter)	23 35
Urn, Roman, found at the Gas Works	94
Vegetius	8
Vertue, Engraver	25
Vespasian, Emperor	5
Vetiones	64
Vettius Benignus, Inscription by	66
Via Julia	8 106 108 110 120
Vibia Jucunda, Inscription to	74
Vicinal Roads	111
Villas, Roman	112
Vosges Mountains	57

W.

	PAGE
Walls of Roman Bath	7
Walls of Mediæval Bath	9
Walcot	30
Wansdike	1 12a
Warleigh, Roman Villa near	119 12b
Warner, Hist. of Bath	vi. 2 12 13 16 17 43 46 47 72 74
Watermore Inscriptions	65
Wellow, Villa discovered there	112 113
Wells	4
Weston Village	5
Whitaker	2 16 17
Whitaker's opinion of Bronze head	26
Wood	vi.
Woodchester, Roman Villa	127
Wookey Hole	4
Wootton-under-Edge, Stone Cist found there containing head of a horse	116
Worship of Roman Emperors	69
Wright, Mr. Thos., (Celt, Roman, and Saxon)	37 63 127
„ Roman mines	30
Wraxall, North, Roman Villa	121 122 123

Y.

	PAGE
Yate, Mr., on mining operations of the Romans	29 30

Z.

	PAGE
Zenodorus of Gaul	27

AQUÆ SOLIS.

THE first origin of the City of BATH is involved in obscurity. That it dates back to a very early period is certain, but whether it was originally a British City, or founded by the Romans when they conquered this part of our Island, must remain in doubt. The pentangular form of the ancient City Walls led Sir R. C. HOARE to suppose that it was of British origin. The Walls, however, appear to have been of Roman construction, if we may trust the researches of Governor POWNALL, who examined a portion laid open in his time, and has described what he saw in a treatise, published towards the close of the last century.[1]

There are many Camps and Earthworks in the neighbourhood of BATH, some undoubtedly ancient British and some Roman: of these notice will be taken hereafter. BATH is situated to the north of the great boundary line called Wansdike, which may be traced from the Woodlands of Berkshire to Macsknoll, not far from Dundry, and which probably continued its course to the Camps on the banks of the Avon, at Clifton, called Stokesley and Borough Walls. Wansdike has been regarded as the Northern boundary of the Belgic territory. PTOLEMY, the Geographer[2], places BATH within that Kingdom. Thus he writes :—

"Τοῖς δὲ Δοβουνοῖς πόλεις καὶ πόλεις,
Ἰσχαλις
Ὕδατα θερμὰ
Οὐέντα."

"Ὕδατα θερμά," or Aquæ Calidæ, can only mean BATH. No other City in this part of Britain can dispute the title.[3]

---

[1] Descriptions and Explanations of some Remains of Roman Architecture dug up in the City of Bath, A.D. 1790; published 1795, 4to.

[2] Claud. Ptolemæi, Geog., lib. 1, c. 7. Mon. Hist. Brit., xv.

[3] Dr. Musgrave says ("Belgium Britannicum," cap. v., § vi.)—"Atque hic, ut opinor, primus harum Aquarum honos, quem mox secquutus est, in domibus, in urbecula condenda labor et opus. Ut orbs Aquarum ergo conditis, sic ab illis Aquæ Calidæ dicta est; a Ptolemæo Ὕδατα θερμά; Claudio, qui Orosus scivit formas nomen imponente. Confuxere (Romani) præsertim devieto jam dedum exercitu Boadiceve (§ vii.) Contra Romanos, cum Siluros, insurgerent, militiæ Romanæ frequentem hac in urbe concursum esse, probabile est; tum Aquarum gratia, tum viæ militaris ad Trajectum (§ ix.)

A

2   ANCIENT AUTHORITIES.

PTOLEMY wrote about A.D. 120: at this period the City was well known as a principal Town within, or just on the Border of the Belgic territory. It might probably be more accurately described as just without the Belgic territory.[1]

In the ITINERARY of ANTONINUS, which was compiled either in the second or the early part of the fourth Century, though the exact date is doubtful, we have mention of "AQUÆ SOLIS" in the 14th Iter., its position being indicated in the route between Isca (Caer-leon) and Calleva (Silchester). It is mentioned again in the ITINERARY of RICHARD of CIRENCESTER (Itinera x., xi., and xii.), whatever authority may attach to that compilation.

In the anonymous RAVENNA LIST, the date of which is probably the seventh Century, we have "Aquis." SOLINUS, who is supposed to have flourished as early as A.D. 80,[2] in a passage which has often been quoted, and is to be found among the extracts which relate to Britain in the "Monumenta Historica Britannica" (Excerpta de Britannia ix.), says:—"Circuitus Britanniæ quadragies octies septuaginta quinque millia passuum sunt. In quo spatio magna et multa flumina, *fontes calidi* opiparo exculti apparatu ad usus mortalium: quibus fontibus præsul est Minervæ numen, in cujus Æde perpetui ignes nunquam canescunt in favillas, sed ubi ignis tabuit, vertit in globos saxeos."[3] This description, which can only relate to BATH, gives some idea of the elegance to which the City must have attained at a very early period.[4]

The Roman Remains which have been found under the site of the present Pump Room, and the vestiges of Roman Baths, amply attest the truth of this representation. From the passage of SOLINUS we gather (as has been observed by Mr. WHITAKER in his Review of Mr. WARNER's "History of Bath," in the Anti-Jacobin Review, Vol. x., 1801), that—

1. The Hot Springs had been collected into elegant basins and furnished with accommodation for the use of Bathers.

[1] See "Archæological Journal," Vol. viii., p. 151, and note.
[2] The date A.D. 80 is ascribed to Solinus by the compilers of the Mon. Hist. Brit., but there is some doubt if he did not live at a later period. Thus Dr. Musgrave, Bel. Brit., vol i., p. 222, Ed. 1719, says,—"Solinus enim non modo diu post Alexandrum Mamæam vixit iquod doctissimus Salmasius ostendit) (Vide illius prolegomena in Solinum) sed et post Ammianum Marcellinum, qui sub Theodosio magno vixit, opinantis non usu rotinac Claudii Christosii." [De vita Amm. Marcellini, ab. Jac. Gronov edit. Log. Bat. 1693.]
[3] Caii Julii Solini Polyhistoria, c. 22, Ed. Salmasii, Trajoct. ad. Rhenum, 1689.
[4] Although, as a rule, no careful antiquary would think of accepting the unsupported testimony of Geoffrey of Monmouth as conclusive on any doubtful point of history, yet it is a curious and impressive fact, that though he is generally supposed to have translated his history into Latin directly, from an original Welsh MS. by Tysilio (a Welsh Bishop, of the seventh Century), yet in his description of Bath he employs terms, especially "in favillas" and "in saxeos globos," which show that either Tysilio or Geoffrey must have been familiar with the description by Solinus, and applied it to the City of Bath, at a time when it is reasonable to conclude that many vestiges of Roman art were still in a state of preservation. The words of Geoffrey of Monmouth are:—"Sustenuit deinde Bladud Siluc, tractaviique regnum vigenti annis: his edificavit urbem Kaerbadum quæ nunc Badus nuncupatur, fecitque in illa callida balnea ad usus mortalium apta, quibus præfecit numen Minervæ: in cujus æde inextinguibiles posuit ignes, qui nunquam deficiebant in *favillas*, sed ex quo tabescere incipiebant, in *saxeos globos* vertebantur."—Geoff. Mon. (Ed. Heideleb., 1587), lib. ii., c. x.

2. The words "Opiparo exculti apparatu" mean even more than elegance, they mount up to magnificence.

3. That Minerva was considered by the Romans as presiding over the Hot Springs, and had a Temple built to her honour.

Altars have been found dedicated to Sul-Minerva, quite confirming this statement, and a Bronze Head, dug up in Stall Street, seems to have belonged to a Statue of that goddess, while the Ægis in the pediment of a Temple (the remains of which are preserved in the Vestibule of the Bath Literary and Scientific Institution), and the figure of the owl which accompanies it, are attributes of Minerva.

4. Fire was kept constantly burning within the Temple, like that in the Temple of Vesta at Rome.

5. The fire never turned to white ashes, as from a wood fire, but "in globos saxeos," (which probably means "into cinders"), and was therefore no doubt fed with coal, which is to the present day dug up at Newton St. Loe, three miles from BATH: a point which is the more noteworthy, since if the interpretation be correct, it is the first mention of the use of coal in Britain.

Several of the Altars discovered in BATH having been dedicated to the Dea Sul or Sul-Minerva, has led some writers on Roman Antiquities to conjecture that the name of BATH must have been Aquæ Sulis and not Aquæ Solis. This was the opinion of the Rev. THOS. LEMAN, as we learn from a MS. note in his copy of the "Britannia Romana," which he bequeathed to the Bath Literary and Scientific Institution. The conjecture is certainly ingenious and not without some authority to support it.

LYSONS assimilates the British deity inscribed on the Altars under the name of *Sul*, to the Roman Minerva, and he is probably right, as Sul is always alluded to as a female divinity; it is always *Deæ* Suli, not Deo Suli. Mr. HUNTER notices this fact.[1] Sir R. C. HOARE thinks that though the word is feminine, it was not equivalent to the Goddess Minerva, but that it is the Celtic *Sol*. Sir RICHARD says[2] "that the name Sul was Celtic there can be no doubt, and it was afterwards latinised into Sol by the Romans, a custom they adopted on many other occasions, and it appears, by the inscriptions preserved at BATH, that they added their own deity, Minerva, to that of the Britons." Mr. HUNTER remarks, on the name being written AQUÆ SOLIS in the ITINERARIES of ANTONINUS and RICHARD, "that the term AQUÆ SOLIS occurs only once in any undisputed remain of Roman times, *i.e.*, in one of the Iters of ANTONINUS, that the authority of RICHARD is doubtful, and

[1] Letter to "Bath Chronicle," June 14, 1827.
[2] "Ancient Wilts," vol. 2.
[3] Letter to "Bath Chronicle," July 19th, 1827

that as ANTONINUS was probably ignorant of the Goddess Sul, and misinformed as to the name of Ancient BATH, and knowing that at the station in question were springs celebrated on account of their natural heat, and being familiar with Heliopolis as a local appellation, he was induced to write Aquæ Solis; or that some early transcriber of ANTONINE, finding Aquæ Sulis, which he could not understand, ventured on his own authority to substitute Aquæ Solis, a name which he could understand, and which appeared to him aptly to describe a place celebrated on account of the natural heat of its waters." These conjectures however probable, are not, to my mind, conclusive enough to enable us to supersede the authority of ANTONINE, who writes the name AQUÆ SOLIS, Sol being a god known to the Romans, and according to St. AUGUSTINE a "Deus Selectus."[1]

In the copy of RICHARD'S ITINERARY, in the Library of the Literary and Scientific Institution, is the following marginal note, in the handwriting of Mr. LEMAN :—"The original name of BATH was Aquæ Sulis, and not Aquæ Solis, the British goddess whose influence extended over the greater part of the south west of England, whose chief place was Solsbury Hill, near BATH, and from whom Salisbury Plains probably derived their name."

SOLINUS, in his description of Britain, mentions also the wealth of the British mines :—"Præterea, ut taceam metallorum largam varismque copiam, quibus Britanniæ solum undique generum pollet vonis locupletibus." This testimony is also confirmed by the remains of lead workings in this county, especially in the Mendip Hills; and by pigs of lead, bearing the Roman stamp, which have been discovered. One pig of lead was found on the site of Sydney Buildings, in BATH, and is now in the Museum of the Literary and Scientific Institution; it bears the stamp of the Emperor HADRIAN, the date being between A.D. 117 and 138. But the earliest date borne by a mass of lead found in Somersetshire is on that discovered in 1853, near Blagdon, in the Blackdown Range, the northern flank of the Mendip Hills. It is now in the British Museum, and the date is from A.D. 44-48. Another of the date of the reign of the Emperor CLAUDIUS, A.D. 49, was found in the time of HENRY VIII., at Wookey Hole, near Wells. The inscription is—

TI. CLAVD. CÆSAR. AVG. P.M.TR.P
VIII. IMP. XVI. DE BRITAN.[2]

These two last mentioned products of the Roman Lead Mines in Somerset show at what an early period this part of the island was brought under tribute. The first of these

[1] See Dollinger's Gentile and Jew, Book vii., part ii.

[2] See Journal of Archæological Institute of Great Britain and Ireland, vol. xvi., pp. 23, 24. Also, Leland's Collectanea, vol. v., fol. 23. Camden Brit., edit. 1607, p. 16d. Dr. Musgrave, Bel. Brit., cap. xvi., § 1. Horsley, B. B., 328.

pigs of lead dates very probably only a year or two after the conquest of this part of Britain by CLAUDIUS, and BATH may be considered as owing its celebrity to the conquests of the Romans in the Reign of that Emperor.

Dr. MUSGRAVE does not hesitate to ascribe to SCRIBONIUS, the physician of CLAUDIUS, who accompanied him in his British campaign, the first adaptation of the hot springs to medicinal purposes, and in this he is followed by Mr. WARNER.

It was A.D. 43 that CLAUDIUS attempted the subjugation of this Island, and sent his lieutenant, AULUS PLAUTIUS, with an army into Britain. VESPASIAN, who commanded the Second Legion, and his son TITUS, served under him in the British War, the events of which are recorded by SUETONIUS and DION CASSIUS.

The testimony borne by TACITUS is as follows :—" Divus Claudius auctor operis, transvectis legionibus auxiliisque, et absumpto in partem rerum Vespasiano : quod initium venturæ mox fortunæ fuit : domitæ gentes, capti Reges, et monstratus fatis Vespasianus." C. C. Taciti Vita Agricolæ, c. 13.

So rapid was the conquest of CLAUDIUS, that he stayed in Britain only 16 days, and was absent from Rome only 6 months, his lieutenant having prepared the conquest for him ; but this did not extend beyond the tract of Britain comprehended within the southern counties, and bounded by the estuary of the Thames and the Severn.

The words of SUETONIUS are—" Claudio principe, Narcissi gratia legatus legionis in Germaniam missus est (Vespasianus) ; inde in Britanniam translatus, tricies cum hoste conflixit. Duas validissimas gentes, superque viginti oppida, et insulam Vectem Britanniæ proximam, in ditionem redegit, partim Auli Plautii consularis legati, partim Claudii ipsius ductu. Quare triumphalia ornamenta, et in spatio brevi duplex sacerdotium accepit."— C. Suetonius Tranquillus, Lib. x., Sive de T. Flavio Vespasiano, c. 4. A.D. 60.

The Belgæ and the Damnonii were the " duas validissimas gentes," and at this time BATH most probably rose into importance.

It does not, however, appear to have been chosen as a legionary station. We have no proof that any legion was quartered here. The Roman funeral monuments to soldiers were probably those of veterans who came for the benefit of the waters, or who having settled here, died in the decline of life. A stone found at Combe Down in 1855 seems to show that there were officers' quarters either there or in some near locality. A small military force was probably stationed in BATH, but neither history nor monumental remains indicate that it was a military station of the same importance as Caer Leon or Chester.

The many Roman villas, the sites of which have been discovered around the City, and which will be treated of in another chapter, serve to shew that the country around was tranquil during a long period, and that great comfort and security prevailed. It seems to have enjoyed a general tranquillity until after the date of the Battle fought at Dyrham, not more than six miles distant from BATH, when the city fell into the hands of the Saxons under Ceawlin, A.D. 577, and probably suffered pillage: the principal buildings being then destroyed, or left in a ruined condition.

We must now proceed to trace the circuit of the city walls, and point out the position of the gates, the direction of the principal streets, and the sites of the chief buildings in Roman times, so far as the Remains hitherto discovered shall enable us.

THE ANCIENT ROMAN WALLS.

THE form of the Roman City seems to have been pentagonal, with four gates facing the cardinal points. The Mediæval Walls were ascertained by Governor POWNALL to be built upon the Ancient Roman foundations, and to have followed the course of the Roman Walls. He states that in 1795 some houses were building on the site of the Borough Walls, opposite the Mineral Water Hospital. The workmen, after they had dug down ten or eleven feet, and laid bare the masonry in the foundation of the Borough Walls, came to that of the Old Roman Walls on which they were set. He states that he examined the different constructions, and satisfied himself that the foundation was clearly *Roman*.

Dr. STUKELEY, whose work[1] was published A.D. 1724, writes of BATH, that the Walls round the City were, in his day, for the most part entire, and perhaps the Old Roman work, except the upper part, which seemed repaired with the ruins of Roman buildings, for the "lewis holes," says he, "are still left in many of the stones; and to the shame of the repairers, many Roman inscriptions, some sawn across to fit the size of the place, are still to be seen, some with the letters towards the city, others on the outside. Most of those mentioned by Mr. CAMDEN and other Authors are still left; but the legend most obscure. The level of the City is risen to the top of the first Walls."[2] The area enclosed by the Walls was about 500 yards E. and W. by 380 yards N. and S., and the direction of the City Wall appears to have been influenced by the nature of the ground. The River Avon protected the City on two sides, and the Walls were adapted to the bend of the River. I am inclined to think that the River at that period approached nearer to the Old Walls than it does at present, and formed a considerable marsh underneath the east and south sides, and was then navigable for small vessels at certain times. There seems reason for believing that in particular localities the courses of the Rivers on which Roman towns were built, have altered considerably since the Roman period, and docks for shipping which were then available are now entirely useless.[3]

[1] Stukeley, Itin. Cur., p. 138.

[2] Leland adds also—"From the S. W. angle has been an additional Wall, and a ditch carried out to the River, by which short work the approach of an enemy on two sides is cut off, unless they pass the River. The small compass of the City has made the inhabitants crowd up the streets in an unseemly and inconvenient narrowness. It is handsomely built, mostly of new stone, which is very white and good."

[3] See Lyell's Geolog. Evid. of the Antiq. of Man, pp. 52, 53.

FORM AND DIMENSIONS OF THE WALLS.

It seems clear that, along the west coast of England and Scotland, there has been a considerable rise of the land. The tide was probably felt as high as AQUÆ SOLIS in Roman times, but the course of the River Avon must have been very similar to what it is at present.[1]

The form of the ancient Walls being pentagonal has led to the supposition that the City was originally British, and dates from before the coming of the Romans. This was the opinion of Sir R. C. HOARE who says :—" We are still enabled to trace the irregular form of the British Town, at Bath, Silchester, Kinchester; while the more regular square and oblong form of the Roman Town may be traced with equal satisfaction at Colchester, Winchester, Caerleon, Castor near Norwich, and in all the Military Stations adjoining the Wall of Severus to the North." Yet we find from VEGETIUS[2] that the Roman Camps did not always follow one figure :—" Interdum autem quadrata, interdum trigona, interdum semirotunda, procul loci qualitas aut necessitas postulaverit, castra facienda sunt :" and I conceive that cities followed the same rule.

COLLINSON[3] says :—"The Old Roman City was built in the form of a pentagon, the area whereof was 1,200 feet in length, and the greatest breadth 1,150 feet. It was surrounded by a strong Wall, composed of layers of stone, brick, and terras, 9 feet thick and 20 feet high. This wall was flanked by circular towers at each angle, and had four gateways, answering nearly to the four cardinal points of the compass, from which, in subsequent times, the principal streets had their denominations."

The great "Foss Road" ran through the Roman City from North to South, entering it through the Porta Decumana at what is now the Eastern angle of the Mineral Water Hospital, and passing down Union Street and through Stall Street, quitted the City at the Porta Flumentana or South Gate, leading to the River. Of the other two Gates the East Gate must have opened upon the River and the Marsh that probably then extended over the flat where the Monk's Mill was erected in mediæval times, and also where Pulteney Street now stands. The Mediæval Gate still exists, at a low level below the Eastern angle of the Market, and the road leading to the Slaughter Houses passes through it. The Roman Gate was probably situated more to the West, and nearer to the site now occupied by the Literary and Scientific Institution. Here it is not improbable that vessels could anchor in Roman times. From the East Gate the Roman Road passed along the Forum, and through the West Gate, following the direction of Cheap Street and Westgate Street, and this Road continued on through the Park until it fell in with the Via Julia which passed through Weston Village.

[1] The Tide is now visible at Hanham, and at Keynsham in extraordinary Tides, but not felt at Bitton, six miles below Bath.
[2] "De Re Militari," lib. 1. ch. xviii.
[3] "Hist. Somerset," vol. I p. 8.

The ancient Forum seems to have occupied the site of the present Abbey Church Yard, as we shall proceed to explain.

Some remains of the Mediæval City Walls still exist. From the East Gate just mentioned, the Wall may be followed for some distance towards the Literary and Scientific Institution, where it runs parallel to the River. Again, at the back of the circular school building attached to Weymouth House, now the Abbey and St. James's Parochial Schools, it is to be traced, although it has unhappily been cased with modern masonry. It is, however, traceable between the Weymouth House School and the Old School belonging to the Roman Catholics, and a considerable remnant of it exists near the Mineral Water Hospital. The circuit of the Walls would be about 55 chains, or 1225 yards, or 3675 feet, and the area contained within them 22½ acres.

JOHN LELAND, the antiquary—who was authorized by HENRY VIII., in the 25th year of his reign, to make a Tour through the Kingdom for the purpose of investigating the national antiquities, more particularly the monastic ones, and collecting charters, deeds, records, manuscripts, &c., from the libraries of the different religious houses,—has recorded what Remains he observed in the Walls of BATH on the occasion of his visit. His words are:—" There be divers notable antiquities engraved in stone, that yet be seen in the Walls of BATH between the South and West Gate, and again between the West Gate and North Gate. The first was an antique head of a man made all flat, and having great locks of hair, as I have in a coin of C. Antius. The second that I did see between the South and the North Gate was an image, as I took it of Hercules, for he held in each hand a serpent. Then I saw the image of a foot-man, *Vibrato gladio et prætenso clypeo*. Then I saw a branch with leaves folded and wreathen into circles. Then I saw two naked images lying along, the one embracing the other. Then I saw two antique heades with hair, as ruffled in locks. Then I saw a grey hound as running, and at the tail of him was a stone, engraved with great Roman letters, but I could pick no sentence out of it. Then I saw another inscription, but the weather had, except a few letters, clear defaced it. Then I saw toward the West Gate, an image of a man embraced with two serpents. I took it for Laocoon. Betwixt the West and North Gate, I saw two inscriptions, of the which some words were evident to the reader, the residue clean defaced. Then I saw the image of a naked man. Then I saw a stone having *cupidines et labruscas intercurrentes*. Then I saw a table, having at each end an image vivid and flourished above and beneath. In this table was an inscription of a tomb or burial, wherein I saw plainly these words, *vixit annos xxx*. This inscription was mostly whole, but very diffusely[1] written, as letters for whole words, and two or three letters conveyed in one. Then I saw two images, whereof one was of a

[1] *i.e.*, Contractedly; the word in the Text is supposed to have been written by Leland in error.

naked man grasping a serpent in each hand, as I took it, and this image was not far from the North Gate. Such antiquities as were in the Walls from the North Gate to the East, and from the East Gate to the South, have been defaced by the building of the monastery and making new walls. I much doubt (he observes) whether these antique works were set in the time of the Roman's Dominion in Britain in the Walls of Bath, as they stand now; or whether they were gathered of old ruins there, and since set up in the Walls re-edified, in testimony of the antiquitie of the Town."[1]

To this interesting record of what existed in the time of Henry VIII., HEARNE adds the following note—" Since Mr. Leland's time there have been also a great number of antiquities discovered at this place, some of which have been carefully preserved and others entirely destroyed. Mr. CAMDEN hath been pleased to account for several, and had he lived to have given us another impression of his book, he would, in all probability, have accounted for many of the rest. . . . . . All I shall note further at present is only to beg leave to insert three Roman Inscriptions that are fixed in the Walls of Bath, which, although that they are already published by Mr. CAMDEN, yet they are very faultily printed there."[2]

HEARNE then gives the following inscription (which will be considered hereafter)—

DEC. COLONIÆ CLEV.
VIXIT AN. LXXXVI.[3]

Also that to SVCC. PETRONLÆ (which will be treated of elsewhere) ; and the fragment of an inscription, with the letters

LIVS SA
IL. VXSO

Which is read

[IV]LIVS SA[BINVS]
[JV]LIAE VXSO[RI]

The S in the second line being doubtless an error of the stone-cutter.

Dr. GUIDOTT and CAMDEN make mention of a little image about a foot and a half in height, supposed by CAMDEN to be Hercules, " having his left hand aloft, with a club in his right ;" and " these letters in a cut stone, very imperfect:"

V. R. N
I O P

[1] See Itinerary of John Leland, vol. 3, (second edition); Oxford 1744; published from the original MS. by Thos. Hearne, M A.
[2] Ibid. Note by Hearne.
[3] See also, A Discourse of Baths, &c., by Thos. Guidott, M.B., p. 69
[4] See Guidott, p. 69.

PLATE I.
SCULPTURES ONCE IN THE WALLS OF BATH,
SELECTED FROM DRAWINGS GIVEN BY GUIDOTT.

GUIDOTT also alludes to "two fierce heads, one within the cope of the Wall, and another to the outside thereof hard by. After that these letters standing overthwart, of which no sense can be made—

IL LA
IL LA

Near this place formerly was a Hare running, now lost. . . . An angry man laying hold of a poor peasant, which may be a bold insulting Roman, on a poor distressed captivated Briton." The same author also mentions the Sculpture of a Shepherd and his Mistress, recognised by the crook in the right hand of the male figure, and the dog fawning upon the woman.[1] "Also a foot soldier brandishing his sword and bearing a shield. A Footman with a truncheon in his right hand. A great face, or a giant's head, with hair. As for Medusa's head all snakes, I cannot (he says), on the best inquiry I can make, find it out. Neither doth Ophiuchus occur to me. 'Tis therefore I believe, lost in the alteration of the Wall, as the Hare, and Medusa's head, mentioned before."[2]

It is to be regretted that all these have perished, or been used as foundations to buildings, where they may lie buried for centuries, and only revive to enlighten some future age, if ever they come to light at all. We can only be thankful that LELAND, CAMDEN, and GUIDOTT have preserved to our times records of what formerly existed. Every fragment becomes more precious as years roll on, and succeeding generations seek to enquire into the habits and manners of past ages. The interest now shown in local antiquities, and the formation of local museums will, we trust, rescue from oblivion whatever may be brought to light in the present or future ages.

We will now leave the Walls to consider what was contained within their circuit, commencing with the probable position of the Forum.

[1] See plate No. 1, page opp. The drawings in which are selected from those given by Guidott and Musgrave, Bal. Brit., cap. vi., § h.

[2] See Guidott, chap. i., 71 and 72.

THE FORUM.

THE principal buildings in Roman Times appear to have stood around the space now occupied by the Abbey Churchyard. On the site of the present Pump Room were discovered the remains of an Ancient Temple. These remains are now in the Vestibule of the Literary and Scientific Institution. An inscription supposed to have been upon the Pediment of the Temple, is also preserved in the Institution, where it has been put up in the passage, and the portions wanting have been supplied, according to a conjectural restoration of the reading by Governor POWNALL. These remains were disinterred A.D. 1790. Immediately fronting this building stood a second Temple, parts of which were, in the course of time, appropriated and adapted as Stalls Church, *i.e.*, the Church of St. Maria de Stabula, or the Virgin at the Manger. This is conjectured from an entry found in an old Book, called "Ruber Codex Bathonies," a MS. on vellum, containing sixty-nine leaves, fairly written on both sides. Mr. WARNER[1] has given a very full account of this Book, which after reciting an epitaph to "Alexander de Alneto et Erneburga uxor ejus," &c., contains the following entry :—

"Est istud epitaphium sculptum a dextra in ostio ruinosi Templi quondam Minervæ dedicati, et adhuc in loco dicto sese studiosis offerens. 1582. 7° Decem. In Civit. Bathon."

The fragments found under the western portion of the present Pump Room may have belonged to this Temple, but it is also probable that the Temple alluded to in this extract formed a distinct building, and that there were two Temples situated on opposite sides of the Forum.

Mr. BRITTON, in his History of BATH Abbey Church, (p. 12) observes[2] :—"An opinion has been very generally entertained that the present Abbey Church of BATH stands on the site of the ancient Temple of Minerva, and this opinion may be clearly traced to CAMDEN'S time."

Dr. STUKELEY, in the year 1724, says—"The Cathedral is a beautiful pile; here they suppose (with probability) stood the Roman Temple of Minerva, patroness of the Baths."[3]

[1] See Warner's Hist. of Bath, app., No. ii., p. 42.
[2] Hist. and Antiq. of Bath Abbey Church; London, 1825.
[3] Itinerarium Curiosum, vol. i., p. 116.

SITES OF TEMPLES. 13

Dr. GUIDOTT, in 1676, speaking generally of BATH, writes thus :—" There is a tradition that there was formerly a temple dedicated to Minerva where now the Church of St. Peter and St. Paul, commonly called the Abbey Church, stands."

CAMDEN says :—" Report tells us there anciently existed a temple sacred to Minerva, where now the Cathedral Church is."

The passage in SOLINUS, asserting that Minerva was the divinity presiding over the BATH Waters, has led to the supposition that both of these Edifices were temples dedicated to her.

The Remains of *two* Edifices, apparently Temples, have been disinterred, and portions of *two* separate inscriptions, apparently belonging to these Edifices, were found with their ruins, but not on the site of the Abbey Church. Of these buildings, one appears to have been the Temple of Minerva, the other that of Diana the Charioteer; at all events, the pediments of the buildings contain the emblems of these divinities. It is not improbable that the site of the present Abbey was occupied by some Roman building, which may have been the Basilica: as we find that on the Continent, Basilicas were usually adapted to Churches, this may have been the case in BATH.

A little to the South West of the Abbey, and between it and the Pump Room, where the remains of the Temple were found, stood the Roman Baths, the foundations of which were discovered in 1755. A particular account of these is given in COLLINSON's History of Somerset (Vol. 1), and has been copied into WARNER's History of BATH.

Accurate plans and drawings were made at the time of the discovery, and Dr. LUCAS and Dr. SUTHERLAND have carefully recorded every particular. We have therefore the actual remains of *three* Edifices, and traditional notice of *two* others, all situated in immediate proximity to the Abbey Churchyard : and running towards it, we have also two principal streets that probably met in the ancient Forum, which formed the centre of the Roman City.

We will now proceed to consider these Buildings separately, and first of all the Ancient *Roman Baths*.

ANCIENT ROMAN BATHS.[1]

ACCOUNTS of the discovery of these Baths have happily been given by successive writers, who have been very careful and minute in their descriptions.

The discovery in the year 1755 attracted particular attention. The portion of the Baths first brought to light was the Eastern Wing, which Dr. LUCAS examined with the assistance of WOOD, the architect: he says it was full 10 feet deep under the Abbey House, and the dimensions of the part then uncovered were 43 feet by 34. "Within and adjoining to the walls are the remains of 12 pilasters, each measuring 3 ft. 6 in. on the front of the plinth, by a projection of 2 ft. 3 in. These pillars seem to have supported a roof. This Bath stood N. and S. To the northward of this room, parted only by a slender wall, adjoined a semi-circular Bath, measuring from E. and W. 14 ft. 4 in., and from the crown of the semi-circle to the partition wall which divides it from the square Bath, 18 ft. 10 in. The roof of this seems to have been sustained by four pilasters, one at each angle, and two at the springing of the circle. This Bath seems to have undergone some alteration ; the base of the semi-circle is filled up to about the height of 5 ft., upon which two pilasters were set on either side from the area, between two separate flights of steps into the semi-circular part, which seems to be all that was reserved for a Bath. In this semi-circular Bath was placed a stone chair 18 in. high and 16 in. broad." To the Bath were two flights of steps, the flight divided by a stone partition, and the steps seeming to have been worn by use three inches and a half out of the square. Eastward of these stairs was an elegant room on each side, sustained by four pilasters. To the eastward of this were other apartments, consisting of two large rooms, each measuring 39 feet by 22 feet.

[1] See Plan.

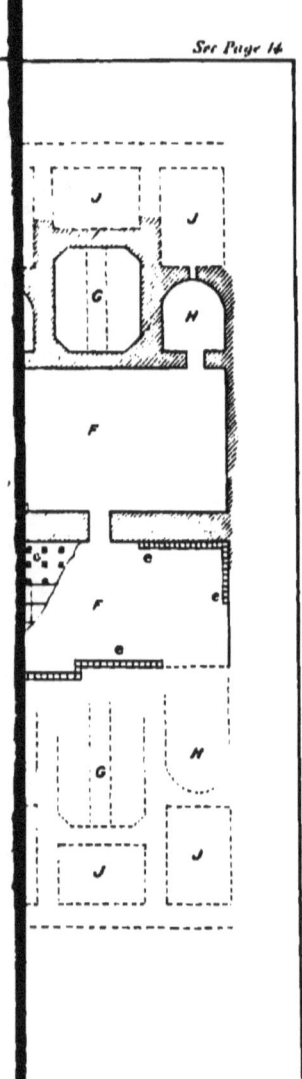

See Page 14

Explanation of the Plan and Section of the ROMAN BATHS, laid open in the City of Bath, in the year 1755, with the Discoveries between the years 1799 and 1803.

A B C D   A Bath, 41 feet long and 34 feet wide.

R R   Two Semicircular Baths.

F F   Two Vapour Baths, whose floors were supported by pillars of brick composition, 1¾ inch thick and 9 inches square, as at c c c, consolidated with strong mortar, about 14 inches asunder; these sustain a floor of strong hard tiles, about 2 feet square, as at d d d d, on which were layers of very firm cement. These rooms were set round with square brick tubes, from 16 to 20 inches in length, as at e e e e.

G G   Furnaces by which the Vapour Baths were heated.

H H H H   Tepid Baths, with Tessellated Pavements.

J J J J J J   Were Dressing Rooms or Antichambers.

K K K K   Part of a larger Bath, 90 feet long and 66 feet wide.

L   Part of a leaden Cistern, containing water of nearly the same heat as the King's Bath.

M   A Channel which conveyed the hot water into the Eastern Square Bath; b b, Channels for conveying water.

N   The Western Bath, corresponding with the opposite side.

O   Supposed to be about the situation of the King's Bath.

P P P P P   The Western side of the Baths, discovered between the years 1799 and 1803.

1, 2, 3, 4   Bases of Pilasters which supported roofs.

a a a a   Steps leading down to the Semicircular Baths.

f f   Drains to carry the water to the River.

The Walls of this magnificent Ruin, when discovered were six or seven feet high, built of stone and mortar, and were lined with coats of red Roman cement, then very firm. The parts more recently exposed were also about the same height, and coated or plastered in the same manner.

"Each had a double floor," *i.e.*, the floors had a hypocaust underneath, and the rooms were heated by means of flues. Remains of the furnace by which they were heated were also discovered, and about the mouth of the furnace were scattered pieces of burnt wood, charcoal, &c., "on each side of the furnace, adjoining the wall of the northernmost stove was a semi-circular chamber of about 10 ft. 4 in., by 9 ft. 6 in. Their floors were nearly 2 ft. 6 in. lower than that of the next stove, into which they both open. The pavements were tessellated with variegated rows of pebbles and red bricks." After the time Dr. LUCAS wrote his description, further discoveries were made of a similar building to the southward, of the same dimensions as the former, and corresponding exactly in position. It was further discovered that these buildings were only the wings of a much larger central building, as is shown in the annexed *plan* taken from Dr. SPRY's Practical Treatise on the BATH Waters.¹ Dr. SUTHERLAND states that "the proprietor of that particular spot in which the left wing of the Roman Baths was built, his Grace the DUKE of KINGSTON, has improved the waters, as far as that space of ground admits of, by erecting six private Bagnios, with corresponding dressing rooms." Thus the Kingston Baths were built upon a portion of the site of the Old Roman Baths, and the passages and walls of these have sometimes been mistaken for the actual Roman Baths.

The length of the foundation traced at successive times after the first discovery was about 245 ft. from E. to W., and the breadth 120 ft. at the broadest part from N. to S. The remains did not long continue open to the public, as modern buildings were soon erected over them. A plan of the Baths was made by Dr. LUCAS, who published a good account of what he saw. This was improved and enlarged by Dr. SUTHERLAND, whose work was published A.D. 1763,² and who in the dedication states that—"In clearing away the foundation of the old Priory, hot mineral waters gushed out, and interrupted the workmen."

Dr. SUTHERLAND states that stone coffins, and bones of various animals, and other things were discovered, which moved curiosity to search still deeper, and the old Roman sewer was at last found, the water drained off. Foundations of regular buildings were also clearly traced.

The finding of Stone Coffins upon the site of the Roman Baths gives the idea that the Baths must have been destroyed at an early period, and that it was by violence rather than the hand of time. No doubt they were standing when the Romans left the Island, about A.D. 420, but betwixt then and the Norman Conquest, the superstructure had

¹ See also the plans in Collinson's Hist. of Somerset, and Gough's edit. of Camden's Brit.
² Attempts to Revive Ancient Medical Doctrines, 2 vols.

been wholly removed, and a portion of the site used as a burial place. It is not improbable that the materials of the Roman Baths were used to build the Saxon Monastery and the Church that accompanied it, and are now buried under the foundations of the noble Abbey Church.

It is hardly necessary to state that WHITAKER, in his review of WARNER's Hist. of BATH, regards this building as at first the residence of the Roman Commander, and afterwards as a Saxon regal Palace. All the remains, however, seem to indicate a magnificent arrangement of Baths, suited to the elegance and luxury of the Roman people, and all writers on the subject agree on this point.

The passage of TACITUS, wherein he describes the gradual enervation of the native character of the Britons through the policy pursued by Agricola, seems particularly applicable to this City.

"Namque ut homines dispersi ac rudes, eoque bello faciles, quieti et otio per voluptates assuescerent; hortari privatim, adjuvare publice, ut templa, fora, domus exstruerent, laudando promptos, et castigando segnes; ita honoris æmulatio, pro necessitate erat. Jam vero principum filios liberalibus artibus erudire, et ingenia Britannorum studiis Gallorum anteferre, ut qui modo linguam Romanam abnuebant, eloquentiam concupiscerent. Indo etiam habitus nostri honor, et frequens toga. Paullatimque discessum ad delinimenta vitiorum, porticus, et balnea, et conviviorum elegantiam; idque apud imperitos humanitas vocabatur, cum pars servitutis esset."[1]

We may conceive of the native Britons occupying Hampton Down (where are vestiges of an ancient British settlement), as looking down upon the Roman town of AQUÆ SOLIS in the valley, and induced gradually to mix with the new comers, to assume their dress and manners, and to become imitators of their luxury.

[1] Tac., Vit. Agric., c. 21.

REMAINS OF THE TEMPLE OF MINERVA.

WE now come to consider the remains, which have been happily preserved to us, of a Temple discovered in 1790, in digging the foundation of the present Pump Room. Many writers have treated of them, and expressed opinions as to the character of the work and the meaning of the design;[1] and Mr. SCHARF, in Archæologia,[2] has done ample justice to these most interesting vestiges.

Mr. WHITTAKER, in a spirited review of the Rev. R. WARNER's History, endeavours to prove that this Temple was in form similar to the Pantheon at Rome, both being dedicated to Minerva. He says: "The Pantheon of Minerva Medica (an agnomen very similar to our prænomen of *Sul* for Minerva) is noticed by RUFUS and VICTOR in their short notes concerning the structures of Rome. . . . In this quarter is still standing a decagon structure. . . . The whole consists of ten sides, in one of which is a door, as in the other nine were as many niches, all of them furnished with as many images of deities. Such (says he) we believe was once the Temple of Minerva at BATH."

In illustration of this subject it may be stated that in the Autumn of the year 1863 the fragments of a Temple, resembling very closely those dug up in BATH, were discovered at Chester. W. TITE, Esq., M.P., who happily had his attention called to them while visiting Chester at the time of the discovery, obtained careful measurements and plans of the structure, and communicated the results of his investigation to the Society of Antiquaries, Jan. 14, 1864.[3] "This Temple consisted originally of 24 Corinthian Columns, 4 at each end, and 8 on each side ; of these 10 remained in their places, *i.e.*, there were 10 Bases and considerable portions of the Shafts. Other fragments of the Shafts and portions of the

[1] Sub hoc tempus urbi accepit Templum Minervæ nuncupatum, quod a Domitiano fervas ædificatum ; certe illa plurimum hale Deæ solebat tribuere, eamqui in testimonio Suetonii superstitions celebat, utpote se illius filium haberi cupiens. (Musgrave Bel. Brit., cap. v., § ix.)

[2] Archæologia, vol. xxxvi.

[3] See Gen. Mag., March, 1864.

Capitals were found in the rubbish, and the foundations of the 24 were to be recognized. Thus the ground plan and elevation could be restored without difficulty. The diameter of the Columns was 2 ft. 3¼ in., and the intervals or intercolumniations about 11 ft. 9 in." The whole structure when perfect must have presented an appearance similar to the Maison Carrée at Nismes.

The diameter of the Roman Column found underneath the Pump Room at BATH nearly corresponds with that at Chester; the BATH Column being 2 ft. 8 in. in diameter, that at Chester 2 ft. 3¼ in. Both Temples were of the Corinthian order of architecture, and they were probably similar in structure. As the Temple at BATH was rather the larger of the two, the intervals of the intercolumniations would be somewhat wider than those of the Temple at Chester, and the appearance of the edifice more imposing. The Temple at Chester, according to Mr. TITE's restoration, was 110 ft. long by 39 ft. 6 in. in width, and the Baths in this instance appear to have been contiguous to the Temple, while at BATH, although situated on the same side of the Forum with the Temple of Minerva, they were thrown further back and occupied the North Eastern portion, the front of each edifice having a Southern aspect. According to Mr. TITE the ruins at Chester are of the same date and character as those found at BATH in 1790.[1]

CORINTHIAN CAPITAL AND BASE, WITH PART OF THE SHAFT.

Of the Remains disinterred from under the present Pump Room the Corinthian Capital deserves the first notice. It has been beautifully drawn in Mr. LYSONS's Book[2] and a restoration of it, together with the Entablature, given.[3] The Capital is executed in a bold masterly style, and seems to be of early date. Its peculiarity is an ornament consisting of small foliage which rises between the volutes and runs over the abacus. Mr. LYSONS observes that the Capitals of the three columns in the Campo Vaccino at Rome, supposed to have belonged to a Temple of Jupiter Stator, have an ornament of the same kind, though richer and more highly finished. The Base and part of the Shaft[4] are of very inferior style, and probably the repairs of a later age. The Base has a groove cut on one side. Mr. LYSONS remarks that—"These fragments, as well as all the other Remains of Roman Architecture, are of the stone dug in the neighbourhood of BATH and still used for building there."

[1] See Bath Chronicle, May 5th, 1864; Report of Literary and Philosophical Association.
[2] Remains of Two Temples and other Rom. Antiq. discovered at Bath; London, 1802. See Plate 1.
[3] Plate 3. Lysons's Rem.
[4] See Plate opposite.

PLATE III.

PEDIMENT OF TEMPLE, AND INSCRIPTION SUPPOSED TO BELONG TO IT.

PLATE II.
CORINTHIAN COLUMN.

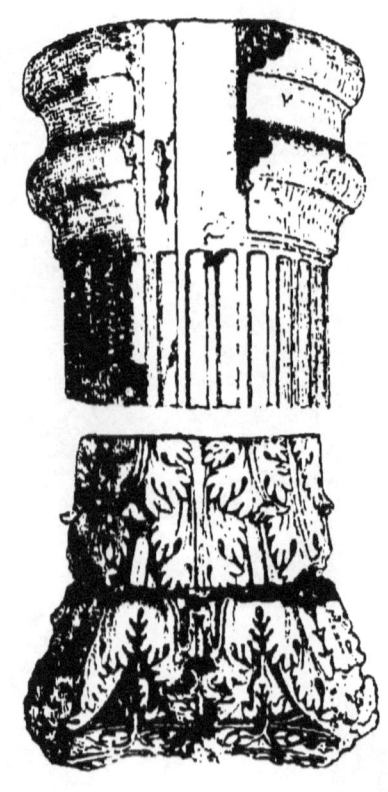

CORNICE AND OTHER FRAGMENTS.   19

A fine Corinthian Capital, but of larger dimensions than that found at BATH, was discovered at Cirencester in 1808. It is described and drawn in Archæologia,[1] and some account of it is given by Professor BUCKMAN and C. H. NEWMARCH, Esq., in their Illustrations of the Remains of Roman Art in Cirencester, the site of Ancient Corinium.[2] This interesting vestige is now deposited in the Park of Miss MASTERS, near Cirencester. It probably belonged to to a Temple, similar in structure to that at Chester; but it is of larger dimensions than either that at BATH or Chester ; for, whereas the Capital of the Cirencester column measures 4 feet across the top, that at BATH is 3 feet 5 in., and the shafts at Chester carried a still smaller Capital. The Temple at Cirencester must, therefore, have been the most imposing building of the three.

CORNICE, AND OTHER FRAGMENTS.

Together with with the Corinthian Capital and Base were found several fragments of a Cornice, richly ornamented with flowers and foliage, consisting of a Cyma Recta, Corona, Ovolo, and Dentils.[3] "As the thickness of the stone, so far as can be presumed from its present condition (observes Mr. LYSONS) would not have been sufficient for the projection of a corner moulding, it is improbable that any was added to the Dentils. The Cornice is considerably less in height than the proportion usually given to that member in the Corinthian order ; but the architect has, in a great measure, obviated this defect, by allowing to every moulding a degree of projection which, when it was in its proper situation, must have tended considerably to remove the appearance of deficiency in height.

The Modillions, which form a part of the usual ornaments of the Corinthian Cornice are here omitted ; but the Corona is made to project six inches and a-half beyond the Ovolo. The Soffit of this projection is richly ornamented with foliage and flowers."[4]

INSCRIPTION ON PEDIMENT.

With these fragments were found some incised stones, forming part of a Friese, with the following portions of an Inscription clearly legible :

....AVDIVS LIGVR .... OLEGIO.
LONGA. SERIA . . . .
E NIMIA VETVS . . . . . VNIA REFICI
ET. REPINGI CVR.. . . ..

[1] Vol., xviii., p. 124, pl. viii.
[2] See p. 19.
[3] See, also, Lysons', pl. ii.
[4] See Plate opposite.

These fragments, with a conjectural restoration of the Inscription by Governor POWNALL, are now placed in the passage of the Bath Literary and Scientific Institution. The restoration is as follows :

[AVLVS CL]AVDIVS LIGVR[IVS SODALIS ASCITVS FABRORVM C]OLEGIO LONGA SERIA [DEFOSSA HANC ÆDEM] E NIMIA VETVS [TATE LABENTEM DE INVENTA ILLIC PEC]VNIA REFICI ET REPINGI CVR[AVIT].

It has been well observed' that—"Restorations of imperfect Inscriptions, although subjects of agreeable speculation, are generally very hazardous, excepting those cases in which the extant words or letters are parts of formulæ, and then a perfectly reliable reading may be supplied from known examples."

The "*sodalis ascitus fabrorum*" was suggested by the expression, "*ex colegio fabrice elatus*," on the stone of JULIUS VITALIS, found in Walcot in 1708, on the side of the Roman road, the ancient Fossway, hereafter to be described.

"*Seria*" was an earthenware vessel, used for burying money (as we know from 2nd Sat. of PERSIUS 11). Many examples have been found here and elsewhere.

E nimia vetustate applies to the dilapidated building, of which it is said—CLAUDIUS LIGUR " *Pecunia refici et repingi curavit.*"

Governor POWNALL's restoration is certainly ingenious if not satisfactory.

Dr. MC.CAUL has observed that *seriæ* were kept in the Temples, and quotes LAMPRID. HELIOGAB. c. 6; but suggests that the true reading is *serie*, or that the final A is a mistake in authography for E. "We have thus," says he, "*longa serie*, and if we supply *annorum*, this phrase and *nimia vetustate* will agree well with *refici et repingi*." In confirmation of this view, he gives two authorities, ORELLI, n. 3,300, and RENIER. Msc. de l'Algérie, n. 109.

Mr. LYSONS ' says:—As much of it as can be restored with a reasonable degree of probability will run thus—

. . [CL]AVDIVS. LIGUR. . . . . . . [C]OLEGIO. LONGA. SERIA [ANNORVM. NEGLECTAM. ET. PR]AE. NIMIA. VETUS[TATE. COLLAPSAM. AEDEM. MINERVAE. SVA. PEC]VNIA REFECI ET. REPINGI CVR[ARVNT].

¹ Britanno-Rom. Inscrip., by Rev. J. McCaul, LL.D., Pres. of Univ. College, Toronto, p. 144.
² See Remains of Two Temples, p. 5.

He further observes that it is plain, from the number of ligatures which occur in the Inscription, that some pains were taken to bring the lines within a certain space; also that it seems probable that the name of some other person preceded that of CLAUDIUS LIGUR, since a greater space remains to be filled up at the beginning than would have been sufficient for a prænomen. "It is probable," he adds, "that another Inscription, expressing by whom this Temple was originally built, ran along the architravo, a fragment of which has the letters VM. remaining on it."[1]

I think we are fairly entitled to gather from these fragments that CLAUDIUS LIGUR (and perhaps another person united with him) restored the Temple and repainted it, after it had been neglected and dilapidated through age, and that this was done at their own cost.

Dr. Mc.CAUL infers a late date for this restoration, from the use of the word *repingi*, a verb which, he says, he does not recollect having seen in any Latin writer earlier than the VI. Cent. A.D. On this, however, it may be observed, that although the "*tied*" or enucleated letters which are common to the Inscription certainly point to a *late* date, yet the Temple is probably at least two centuries earlier than the date suggested by Dr. Mc.CAUL.[2]

TYMPANUM OF PEDIMENT.

The Tympanum of the Pediment,[3] discovered at the same time with the other remains, calls for especial notice. In altitude it measured 8 feet 4 inches, and in length 24 feet 2 inches. This Sculpture belongs to the age of the decadence of the arts, but is not inferior in execution to some of the works of its period found in Rome. "The execution is coarse, and the material, taken from the quarries in the neighbourhood, does not admit of great delicacy of execution. The eyes are crude, and extravagant in drawing; but there is an effective treatment of the work, as intended for a distance, and a peculiar roundness about the flesh. The arrangement of the hair is very artistic, and the mode in which the snakes are made to combine with it is worthy of observation. It must have originally consisted of twelve stones, only six of which remain. The subject is a large circular shield, called "clipeus," supported by two flying figures of Victory. The feet of the right hand Victory still remain attached to a globe."[4] Governor POWNALL endeavoured to prove that this head was the "serpentine, or cherubic diadem, which the Egyptians, Rhodians, and some other nations in the east, placed upon the head of the divine symbol of their god."

[1] See Rem. of Two Temples, p. 5.
[2] See B. R. Inscrip., p. 164.
[3] See plate on opp. page. See also an excellent drawing by Mr. Scharf, in Archæol. XXXV., p. 190; plate 36.
[4] Archæologia, XXXVI., p. 189

Some, like Mr. CARTER, have considered it to be the head of Medusa. Mr. BRITTON, in a note upon a recent edition of CARTER (1838), said it was intended to represent the ægis of Minerva. The ægis was originally a *goat-skin*; and when Jupiter was contending with the Titans, he was directed to wear it, with the head of the Gorgon. HOMER designates Jupitor, Αιγιοχος (ægis-bearing); and from this circumstance the goat-skin became the mantle or paludamentum of the Roman emperors; whereas the Medusa's head at last degenerated into a mere fibula or button, with which the cloak was fastened to the right shoulder.

The ægis was therefore quite *distinct* from the shield of Minerva; and the object now under consideration is a *shield* of a large round "clipeus" form, supported by figures of Victory. Between the head and the rim of the shield are two circles or wreaths of oak-leaves and acorns. These have no direct reference to Minerva. "May it not be," asks Mr. SCHARF, "that this head is the symbol of the hot spring, and that the double wreath refers to the oak groves which may have surrounded the locality"?

Minerva was, according to SOLINUS, the presiding divinity,—"quibus fontibus præsul est Minerva numen." Two altars are now standing in the entrance passage of the Literary Institution, dedicated to the goddess Sul-Minerva, two to the goddess Sul, and one to the Sulevæ. There is also a memorial stone, put up to a *priest of the goddess Sul*. Another fragment of an inscription, which reads

C. PROTACI
DEÆ. SVLIS. M.

is still preserved, and seems to have belonged to a distinct Templo. It appears probable from this, that the Romans, finding the worship of the goddess Sul established here, and, it may be, conducted on the hill called Salisbury (still bearing a corruption of her name), added to it that of their *own* Minerva, under the title of "Sul-Minerva," and regarded this goddess as presiding over the hot springs, and erected to her a noble Temple, of which the Pediment and one Column now alone remain.[1]

The central head in the shield may be, as Mr. SCHARF observes, a personification of the hot spring itself. The abundant curls indicate the flowing streams; and the wings just above the ears may relate to the fleeting and evanescent nature of the BATH waters, which, from their intense heat, quickly evaporate. If this view be correct, the locality of the hot

[1] It is worthy of remark, that near Ribchester (Coccium), where considerable remains of a Temple dedicated to Minerva are said to have been found, is a spot called "Salsbury." See Camden, Gough's edition, vol. iii., p. 379.

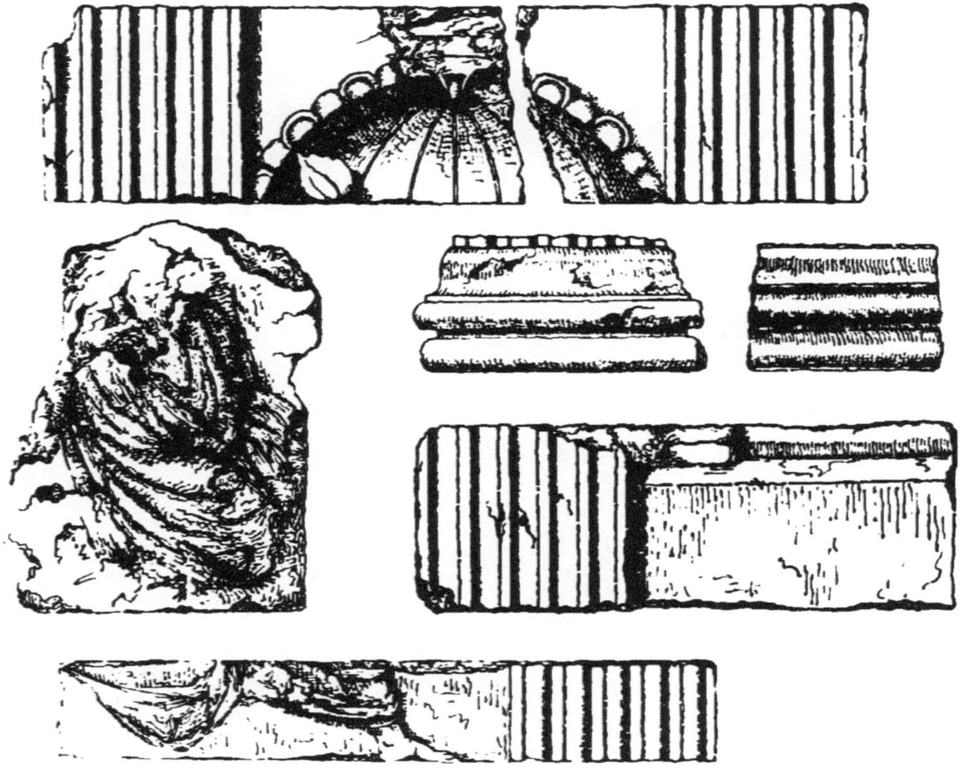

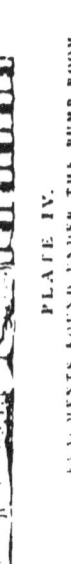

PLATE IV.

FRAGMENTS FOUND UNDER THE PUMP ROOM.

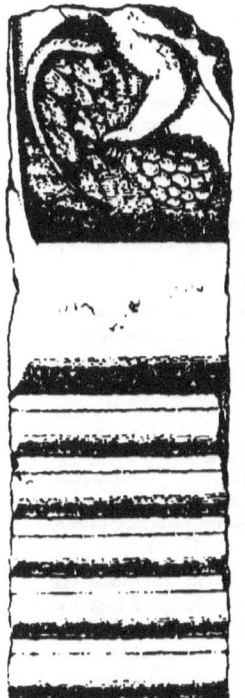

PLATE V.
FRAGMENTS OF SCULPTURES OF THE SEASONS.

spring being in a valley, we may have it typified in the *deeply concave* form of a "clipeus" around the head and circle of oak-leaves; whereas all bucklers in ancient art partake of the opposite, or convex, form. Surely the BATH waters, or their supposed divinity, deserved a temple; for to these the city owes its continuance through all periods of history, while others, like Uriconium, Kenchester, and Silchester, have quite passed away, or become unimportant places.

At the left hand corner of the Pediment is a helmet of a very peculiar, and, in Mr. SCHARF's opinion, unclassic shape. On the right hand side above, is part of an arm with a bracelet; and below it is a hand holding a wreath belonging to a flying Victory. Lower down is the hand of a child holding an owl by the wing. More is an emblem of Minerva and of Night also; the helmet may be regarded as allusive to Mars, and would have an appropriate allusion in a Roman colony; and equally suggestive would be the owl of Minerva, the goddess presiding over the hot springs; for, as remarked by PROCLUS, a very late Greek author, who died A.D. 485—

'Η ΑΘΗΝΑ ΝΙΚΗ προσαγορευεται και ΥΓΙΕΙΑ, το μεν ινα κρατιω τινωτα της ανοητος, και το ιδος της υλης, ιλεω δαιει και τελειον, και αγηρων, και ανοσω διαφυλαττουσα το παν, οικειω ευν της του θεου ταυτης, και αναγειν, και μεριζειν, και δια της νοερας χορειας ευναπτειν τοις διωτεροις, και ιδρυειν και φρουρειν εν αυτοις.

Thus translated:

Minerva is called Victory and Health: the former because she causes intellect to rule over necessity, and form over matter; and the latter because she preserves the universe perpetually whole, perfect, exempt from age, and free from disease. It is the property, therefore, of this goddess to elevate and distribute, and through an intellectual dance, as it were, to connect, establish, and defend, inferior natures in such as are more divine.

On each side of the shield is the fragment of a flying Victory. The folds of the drapery of the left hand figure are well arranged, and the feathers are distinct in form. A similar arrangement to that of the supporting figures in this sculpture is to be seen on a fragment found at Lanchester, and now placed in the entrance to the library of the Dean and Chapter at Durham. Each Victory stands on a globe, and has a shield on her arm. Circles or bands like those upon the globe under the feet of the right hand figure of the BATH sculpture also occur in paintings at Pompeii, and on coins of AUGUSTUS.

Fluted pilasters, and the remains of four small sculptures of the Seasons, were also disinterred from the same spot (the site of the present Pump Room), and are preserved in the vestibule of the Literary Institution. The sculptures are faithfully given by Mr. LYSONS in his engravings, and out of the fragments he has ideally constructed a small temple.

The Head in the Pediment[1] has hitherto been considered to be that of the goddess *Sul*, in consequence of a portion of an inscription found with it, which runs thus—

C. PROTACI
DEÆ SV.IS M

And has been restored thus—

C. PROTACIVS
DEÆ SVLIS MINERVÆ.

" C. Protacius, to the goddess Sul Minerva."

Two small cells or chapels seem to have stood one on each side of the larger Temple. Mr. SCHARF supposes them to have formed parts of the larger structure. One of these has been reproduced by Mr. LYSONS from the fragments which remain.[2] He says—"The fragments collected have afforded sufficient authority to produce the whole of the restoration, except the Entablature, of which there are no remains. The extent of the front is ascertained by the Tympanum of the Pediment, a great part of which remains. It extends 17 feet, and allows the intercolumniation to be 2½ feet in diameter." He supposes this small Temple to have been dedicated to Sul-Minerva, but the remains rather show it to be a small Temple of Luna or Selene. The goddess is represented full-faced, with the crescent, not on her forehead, but behind her head, gracefully filling up the circular space. The right shoulder is bare, on the left is her whip, and her hair is tied in a knot over her forehead, in accordance with other classic representations of the virgin goddess.

I am inclined to agree with Mr. WARNER and Mr. SCHARF, that this must be the remains of a structure representing the goddess Luna ; but I cannot quite agree with Mr. SCHARF that, although found in the same spot, it belonged to the large Temple. Part of a medallion representing the Sun was also found at the same time ; but of the rays, which seem not to have exceeded seven in number, part only are left. " The remaining edge of this medallion corresponds (says Mr. SCHARF) in size with that of the Moon or Selene"; and from this he infers that they were portions of two corresponding smaller Pediments. He supposes also that the Sculptures of the Seasons were portions of the decorations of the large Temple, and that the figure on the Pediment represented the presiding deity of the Hot Springs.

[1] Amongst the ruins at Caerleon was found a sculpture, with a head resembling that discovered at Bath, but of much inferior workmanship. See Engraving in Mr. Lee's descriptions of a Roman building, and other remains discovered there, published in 1850. Plate viii.

[2] See Plates vi. and vii. ; also, pp. 5, 6, 7.

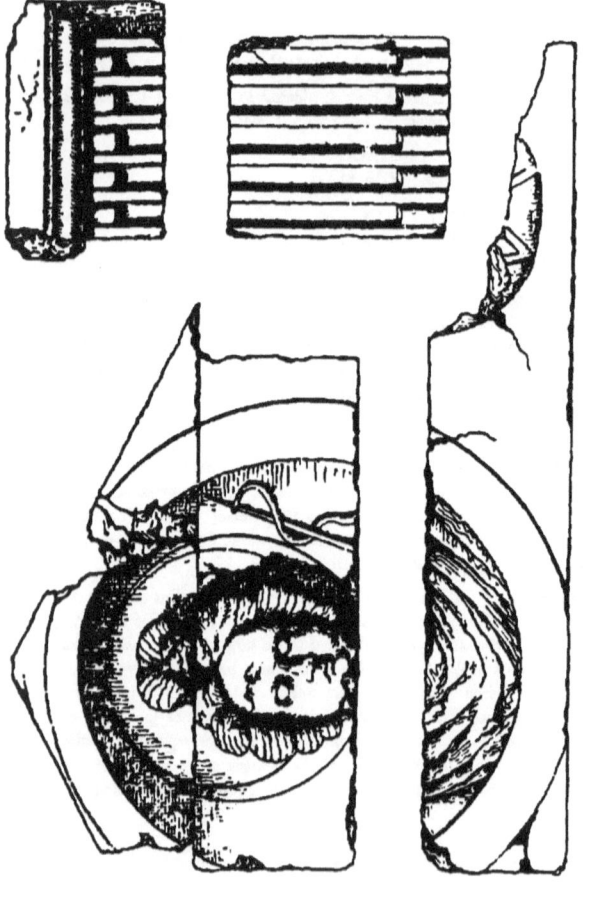

PLATE VI.

HEAD OF LUNA, WITH FRAGMENTS AND INSCRIPTION TO [illegible]

The discovery of so many Roman Remains at one time and in one spot, suggested to the Corporation of BATH the propriety of forming some depository for such evidence of the former importance of the city, and a Museum was formed in Bath Street in the year 1790.[1] From this Museum all the fragments discovered under the Pump Room, with the Remains previously found, were afterwards removed to the Literary and Scientific Institution, by an order of the Mayor, Aldermen, and Common Council, in January, 1827.

THE BRONZE HEAD OF PALLAS.

This was found 20th July, 1727, in digging a sewer in the centre of Stall Street, about 15 feet deep in the ground. It formerly stood in the Town Hall, but is now placed in the inner Library of the Literary and Scientific Institution. It is considered one of the most interesting reliques found in this island. Drawings of it, which were made at the time of its discovery, are now in the Literary and Scientific Institution. By permission of the Mayor and Corporation, Sir H. ENGLEFIELD caused a cast of this Head to be made and presented to the Society of Antiquaries of London, May 30, 1799. In his opinion the Head had been re-gilt some years previously, but he supposed that traces of the original gilding remained.

The Head appears to have been broken off from a Statue, the neck bearing evidence of violence in the uneven and ragged outline ; and there are perforations in the upper part of it showing that some ornament was formerly fixed upon it above the hair. What this ornament was, may probably be conjectured from a drawing of a Terra Cotta Head of Pallas Athene, from CALVI, engraved in Mr. BIRCH'S Ancient Pottery and Porcelain,[2] which in expression much resembles the Bronze Head : it may, however, have been a helmet. VIRTUE engraved a representation of the Head in 1730,[3] and when HORSLEY visited BATH, 1730, it stood in the Town Hall, where also was preserved a Box of Coins, which were found at the same time.[4] The Coins were of the Emperors—

M. AURELIUS,
MAXIMINUS,
MAXIMIAN,
DIOCLESIAN,
CONSTANTINE, and some others.

[1] It is much to be regretted that, in consequence of this step not having been taken at an earlier period, so much that is known to have existed has been irretrievably lost.
[2] Vol. I., p. 169.
[3] See pl. xxxiv. of Vet. Mon., vol. i.
[4] See Brit. Rom., p. 329.

It has been a subject of dispute whether the Head is that of Apollo or Minerva. HORSLEY seems to incline to the former opinion, Mr. HUNTER to the latter.[1] Mr. WARNER confidently assigns it to Apollo. He says—"It is a beautiful fragment of a Statue of Apollo, which stood probably in a Temple dedicated to him, near the spot where the Head was discovered. That this Deity should have a Temple raised to his honour in a city which received its appellation from himself (Aquæ Solis) will scarcely admit of a question, particularly as he was esteemed to be potent in the infliction and cure of many disorders." On the other hand, Mr. WHITAKER[2] says—"The form of it is very fine, and the features are truly Minerva's. This military goddess has been expected by some to be like Venus, the goddess of smiles and love. She is a goddess very different, wearing a helmet on her head, woilding a javelin in her hand, even carrying a Gorgon's head of snakes upon her breast-plate, and thus mixing in fight with men. So acting, she must of necessity show a manliness and muscularity in the face, superior, perhaps, to any even in the Belvedere Apollo." Mr. WHITAKER supposes the date of the Head to have been betwixt A.D. 161 and 181.

The discovery of the Head not far from the ruins of the Temple under the Pump Room, leads to the supposition that the statue may have been placed in that Temple.

Another Head is said to have been found in BATH. This was purchased by the late Mr. PIGOT, of Brockly Hall: a cast of it is now in the Institution, and there is also one in the British Museum. No mention, however, has been made of it by any of the writers on BATH Roman antiquities, nor was it ever entered in the catalogue of Roman remains discovered in the city, although Dr. SPRY[3] states that it was found when the site of the Roman Baths was uncovered, adding that it is supposed to be the head of Diana, and that it was in the possession of the late Mr. HOARE.

The cast of a small marble statue of Minerva, about 2 ft. 7 in. high, which is also said to have been found in BATH, was bequeathed by the late PRINCE HOARE, Esq., F.S.A., to the Society of Antiquaries, and is mentioned in their Proceedings.[4] The statue was exhibited in the Museum of the Somersetshire Archæological and Natural History Society, formed on the occasion of their meeting at BATH, in 1852,[5] but it is not mentioned in the

---

[1] See Cat. of Antiq., L. and S. Ins., p. 86.
[2] See Hi. of B. R. A., No. xiii., p. 89.
[3] Anti-Jacobin Review, vol. 10, p. 346.
[4] See "Practical Treatise on the Bath Waters," by Joseph Hume Spry. 1822.
[5] Vol. xxvii., p. 5. See also Catalogue of Collection of Antiquities, Coins, Pictures, &c., in possession of the Society of Antiquaries. London, 1847; compiled by Albert Way, Esq., F.S.A.
[6] See "Proceedings," p. 16, 17.

PLATE VII.
ROMAN FEMALE HEAD FOUND IN BATH, NOW WALLED INTO THE
PORCH OF A HOUSE IN MUSGRAVE'S ALLEY, EXETER.

PLATE VIII.
ROMAN PIG OF LEAD.

Literary Institution Catalogue of Antiquities, nor by any writer on BATH Roman Antiquities, and I have been unable to obtain any satisfactory information respecting it.

The Remains in Bronze which have been found in London as well as the Bronze Head found in BATH serve to show that the art of Casting in Bronze had been carried to great perfection in this Island during the Roman occupation, and quite confirm the words of PLINY.[1] Mr. ROACH SMITH, in his "Illustrations of Roman London,["] has given drawings of the Bronzes found in London or dredged up from the bed of the Thames. They are of beautiful workmanship, and the few that have been preserved lead us to regret that many works of Roman art which must have formerly existed in this country, have perished for want of interest in their value. The Head of the Emperor HADRIAN, the colossal bronze Hand, 13 inches long, which had been broken off from a statue of about the same magnitude as that from which the Head of HADRIAN had been severed, and probably forming part of a statue of the same Emperor, all evince a high state of art at the period of that Emperor. "Among the workers in metal of that epoch," observes Mr. ROACH SMITH, "was Zenodorus in Gaul, who fabricated in that province many works of great merit; and among them a colossal statue of Mercury for the city of Averni; and at Rome a statue of NERO one hundred and ten feet high. The bronze statue of ANTINOUS, heroic size, found at Lillebonne, between Rouen and Havre, figured in vol. iii. of the Collection of Antiquities, and now preserved in the Louvre, may be appealed to as an example of the style of the school to which the Head of HADRIAN belongs; also the Head of Apollo found at BATH, and a fragment of a leg and hoof of a horse found at Lincoln, and preserved in the collection of the Society of Antiquaries at Somerset House." We may hence infer that the date of the Head of Pallas, which Mr. ROACH SMITH considers to be Apollo, is about that of the Emperor HADRIAN. A pig of lead, with the stamp of that Emperor, was found in Sydney Buildings, Bathwick.

COLOSSAL FEMALE HEAD, CARVED IN BATH STONE.

In the year 1714 this Head was discovered in BATH, and sent by Mr. FRANCIS CHILD as a present to Dr. MUSGRAVE, who then resided in Exeter. Dr. MUSGRAVE named it the Britanno-Belgic Andromache, and caused it to be set up in the porch of his house.[3] The statue of which it formed part must have been 8 ft. 2 in. high. It probably stood upon a pedestal or perhaps a column, and (as Mr. HUNTER supposes) gave Mr. LYSONS the hint of the obelisk crowned with a statue, which he has introduced in his general view of what BATH may have been in the most flourishing times of Roman grandeur.[4]

[1] Nat. Hist., lib. xxxiv., c. 7, 8.
[2] Plates xv. to xxii., and frontispiece.
[3] See Dr. Musgrave's Bel. Brit., vol. I., chap. xix.
[4] See Frontispiece to Remains of Two Temples.

It afterwards fell into the possession of Mr. LUKE, a Solicitor in Exeter, who occupied a house in Musgrave's Alley, said to have formerly belonged to Dr. MUSGRAVE, and it is built into the wall of the porch, so as to show both the back of the head and the front face.' The plate of it in Dr. MUSGRAVE'S Book is a very fair representation, excepting that the arrangement of the hair in the sculpture is more natural than in the engraving, and the head-dress, instead of being a sort of diadem, seems more like a well-curled wig.

In the sculpture the hair sets off from the head by the cheek, as natural hair would do, so that the hand may be put underneath, and the circles are not so even and true, nor so flat as in the drawing, but rounded more like natural curls. There are two twisted locks of hair which come somewhat over the face.

Dr. MUSGRAVE supposes the head-dress to represent the style prevalent in the time of the Emperor DOMITIAN, and (with the remark, "Qua mulierum in vestitu enormitates scriter perstringit") applies to it the lines of JUVENAL, Sat. vi.

'Tot premit ordinibus, tot adhuc compagibus altum,
Ædificat caput, Andromachon a fronte videbis,
Post minor est, credas aliam.'

He considers it to be of the date A.D. 81, when AGRICOLA commanded in Britain. A drawing of this Head is given by HORSLEY.' It is also described in COLLINSON'S History of Somerset,² and WARNER'S History of BATH,⁴ where it is wrongly supposed to have come into the possession of Lord PEMBROKE, and been carried to Wilton. It is much to be regretted that it has passed out of the City of BATH, as it ought to form part of the Collection of Roman Antiquities in the Literary and Scientific Institution. A Writer in the "Bath Chronicle," 27th Sept., 1862, suggests a hope that it may yet be obtained by the City.

[1] Through the courtesy of Mr. Lahm, since deceased, I saw this Head in 1859.
[2] B. R.; see p. 229.
[3] Vol. 1, p. 14.
[4] p. 29, and "Illustrations;" Introduction, p. 26.

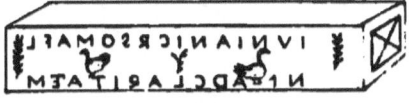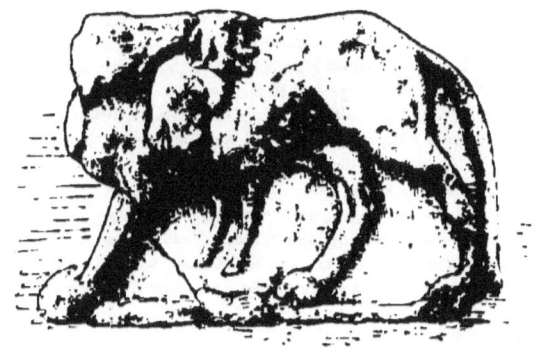

PLATE IX.
MEDICINE STAMP, AND SCULPTURE OF A DOG CARRYING A DEER
FOUND IN BATH ON THE LINE OF THE FOSS ROAD.

ROMAN METALLURGY.

A Pig of Lead, bearing the stamp of the Emperor HADRIAN,

IMP. HADRIANI. AVG.

was discovered, A.D. 1822, near Sydney Buildings, S.W. of Sydney Gardens, in the course of works under the direction of Mr. GOODRIDGE, Architect, BATH, by whom it has been deposited in the Literary and Scientific Institution. An ancient Key found with the Pig of Lead is now deposited with the other BATH antiquities in the Museum. The Pig of Lead, which weighed 1 cwt. 83 lbs., is mentioned by the Rev. W. PHELPS.[1]

Mr. YATE,[2] in a very interesting paper on "The Mining Operations of the Romans," states that "it bears exactly the same Inscription as those from Snailbeach, Shelve, and Snead, so that it may reasonably be presumed to have come from the Shropshire Mines. In its size and form it also agrees remarkably with those specimens." I should rather incline to think that it was the product of the Mendip Mines, which were worked much earlier by the Romans than those in Shropshire: probably, however, in the reign of HADRIAN one uniform stamp prevailed for all the Mines under the Roman dominion in Britain.

The Lead bearing a Roman stamp discovered in Somerset is the earliest of any found in our Island.[3] That found August, 1853, near Blagdon, Somerset, probably dates as far back as A.D. 48 ; that at Wookey, near Wells, A.D. 49. Thus the Mendip Mines were worked as early as the time of CLAUDIUS by the Romans, or at all events the produce of the Mines then in work was put under tribute, and received the Emperor's mark. The date of the Pig of Lead found in BATH is between A.D. 117—138 ; some 80 or 90 years later.

[1] Hist. Som., vol. I, p. 161 ; Journal of Brit. Arch. ap., vol. v., p. 226 ; Archæo. Journal, xvi., p. 34 ; and Som. Arch. and N. H. Soc. Proceedings, vol. viii., p. 15.
[2] Som. Arch. and N. H. Soc. proceedings.
[3] See Arch. Journal, vol. xvi., p. 23, 24.

At Charterhouse-on-Mendip abundant traces of Roman Mining have been observed, and the appearance of the hills in the vicinity of the Mines corresponds with that which Mr. THOMAS WRIGHT describes as occurring at Shelve, in Shropshire, viz., "the excavations take the form of vast caverns, which have gone to a great depth, but the entrance has been clogged up with fallen rock." Mr. WRIGHT supposes that the Roman Miners "began at the bottom" of the hill, where they observed the veins to crop out, and having "followed the metal in one spot as far as they could, they commenced immediately above, and filled up the previous excavation with the waste from the new one."

At Charterhouse-on-Mendip,[1] near the site of the Roman Station, is a perfect Roman Amphitheatre, and about half-a-mile distant from it there are traces of another, which has been partially filled up. These are noticed by Sir R. C. HOARE[2] in his survey of the Roman road which passed the Roman Station at Charterhouse-on-Mendip and led from Old Sarum (Sorbiodunum) to the Roman Port on the Severn at Brean Down (Ad Axium). I have in my possession three Roman Coins[3] picked up at Charterhouse, and Mr. YATE mentions a copper coin of ANTON. PIUS. He says "large heaps of slag have been found, still rich in lead, so as to prove that the Romans were not successful in the extraction of the metal from its ore, also a quantity of the ore finely pounded, so as to be ready for smelting, and in the state now known by the name *slimes*. . . There are several grooves cut in the mountain from which the ore was doubtless extracted. Some remarkable implements of wood, and a powerful iron pick-axe were found at Luxborough, not far from Dunster, where it appears that the Romans had iron-mines and made use of the Brown Hematite." Drawings of these mining implements are given.[4] The originals are preserved in the Museum of the Society at Taunton.

The Foss Road from BATH to Ilchester cuts the Roman Road from Old Sarum to the port on the Severn (probably the Ad Axium of the Ravenna List), not far from an ancient camp called Maesbury Castle. Both lines of road are laid down in the map of the Ordnance Survey, and the point of contact of the two is near Oakhill. By these Roads such part of the produce of the Mines of Mendip as was needed for use in the city or province, would be brought to AQUÆ SOLIS.

Near the spot where the Roman Pig of Lead was found, some interments have since been discovered. In January, 1861, two stone coffins were exposed. One contained the skeleton of a young female imbedded in fine white sand, which, on being

[1] For acct. see Archæol. Journal, vol. xvi., p. 153.
[2] Ancient Wilts, vol. ii. Roman Æra.
[3] One Probus, two Tacitus; one of them being a copper coin plated.
[4] Som. Arch and Nat. Hist. Soc. Proceedings, vol. viii., p. 16, pl. 11.

submitted to careful microscopic examination, was found to be similar in composition to that obtained from the mineral veins which produce Lead ore in Mendip, and no sand of the same description is found nearer to BATH than the Mendip Hills. From this it seems probable that not only Lead Ore, but sand for the purpose of interments, was procured from the Mines. A more particular account of these interments will be given hereafter.

ROMAN MEDICINE STAMP.

IT is most probable that a School of Medicine existed in BATH at an early period. The Mineral Springs being visited by many patients for their healing benefits, would naturally cause the residence of eminent Physicians in the neighbourhood. No record, however, has been found of any patients, nor have we any Votive Altar put up by a Physician, as at Chester, or any memorial to a Physician, as on the line of the Roman Wall in Northumberland.

A solitary Medicine Stamp is all that has been discovered to indicate the practice of Medicine in BATH in Roman times, and it seems probable that this was the Stamp of an Empiric. This Medicine Stamp was dug up in the Abbey Churchyard in 1731, in making a cellar. It passed into the possession of Mr. MITCHELL, of Bristol, about the middle of the last century, but it cannot now be traced. It was a stone of greenish hue, perforated, and of oblong form. At the time of the discovery it was shown to the Society of Antiquaries, and casts of the impressions upon it were presented to that body by Mr. LETHIECULLIER: three of them are still preserved in their Museum.[1]

In 1788, Mr. GOUGH published in Archæologia,' "Observations on certain Stamps and Seals used anciently by oculists." Dr. SIMPSON, of Edinburgh, has also done much to elucidate the reading of the Inscriptions on this Stamp[2]; and Dr. McCAUL, president of University College, Toronto, has, with much learning and critical acumen, suggested very probable emendations in the former readings.[3]

The legends on the four sides are as follows :—

1. T. IVNIANI THALASAR AD CLARITATEM.
2. T. IVNIANI CRVSOMAEL IN M AD CLARITATEM.
3. T. JVNIANI DIEXVM AD VETERES CICATRICES.
4. T. JVNIANI PHOEBVM AD LV ECOMA DELICTA A MEDICIS.

[1] MS. notices of this Stamp are preserved in the Min. Book of the Soc. of Antiq., vol. iv. (1714), p. 210; and vol. viii. (1757), p. 29.
[2] See Edinburgh Med. Journal, March, 1861.
[3] See Brit. Rom. Inscrip., p. 176.

I have here given the amended readings, as the two last Inscriptions seem to have been copied imperfectly, and are therefore doubtful. In No. 3, the initial letters of the last word are in a rude Britanno-Roman character, and their meaning can only be conjectured. The plaster cast of this side has been lost.

Dr. SIMPSON observes that the "fourth legend appears the most puzzling of all the Inscriptions hitherto found upon the Roman Medicine Stamps discovered in Britain." The word, however, after the name of the Vendor of the Medicine, T. JVNIANVS, appears to be PHOEBVM.

To add to the difficulties of interpreting this stone, the spelling of the original has been executed very carelessly by the engraver. Thus, in No. 2, we have CRSOMAELINVM for CRYSOMELINVM; and in No. 1, THALASER for THALLASSER.

In No. 4, the word LEVCOMA has been read QVECVMO, but Dr. McCAUL suggests QVECVMQVE, the E being used for Æ and the final Q for QVE.

In No. 4, PHOEBVM has also been read PHORBIVM. The Phorbium, according to GALEN, "possesses attenuating, attractive, and discutient powers. They apply its Seeds, mixed with honey, to Leucoma, and it is believed to have the power of attracting Spicula of Wood."

The word DELICTA is conjectured by Dr. McCAUL to be RELICTA, and used for *derelicta*, as in Orelli, n. 1518. Thus the word would admit of two interpretations, either "badly treated" or "given up" by the Physicians.

The Stone may therefore read thus—

1. The Thalasser of TITUS JUNIANUS for Clearing the Eye-sight.
2. The Crysomelinum of T. JUNIANUS for Clearing the Eye-sight.
3. The Diexum or Dryxum of T. JUNIANUS for Removal of Old Scars.
4. The Phœbum (or Blistering Collyrium) of T. JUNIANUS for such hopeless cases as have been given up by the Physicians.

The name on each of these Stamps is that of a Collyrium, or Eye Salve.

The DIEXVM, or DRYXVM, or DRVCVM, probably from δρυς, an oak, may have been composed of gall nuts, and used as an astringent.

The name PHOEBVM is not known as a Collyrium, but PHORBIVM was used by the Ancients; or the word, as Dr. McCaul observes, may be PHOEDVM, the Latinized form of ΦΟΙΔΟΝ or ΦΩΔΟΝ, derived from φωζω. If the word be PHOEBVM it is used in the sense of "Radiant" or "Appollinarian."

Other Medicine Stamps have been found in this country, as at Cirencester [1] and Wroxeter.[2] Dr. McCaul observes that, of the Roman Remains scattered over Europe, probably none present greater difficulties to the antiquary than Medicine Stamps. The subject has, however, been explained and illustrated by Spon, Chishull, Caylus, Saxe, Walche, Gough, Tochon, Sichet, Duchalais, Way, and Simpson, as well as in the work of Dr. McCaul on Roman Inscriptions, whence much of the explanation which is here given has been obtained.

[1] See Corinium, by Prof. Buckman and Mr. Newmarch.
[2] Archæol Journal, vol. xvi., p 66.

SCULPTURE OF A DOG CARRYING A DEER.

A Stone with a Sculpture in bas-relief, representing a Dog carrying a Deer, was found about five years ago on the line of the Foss Road as it passes through Walcot into BATH. Here also were found the Julius Vitalis Monument and several remains of Roman Interments. The Sculpture now under consideration was dug up in preparing the foundations for a house. It seems to have formed the upper portion of a Tomb, and is probably Roman, although this is merely conjectural, as there is no lettering or Inscription by which its use or age can be determined. The Sculpture represents a well formed and vigorous Hound, carrying a Roe-deer, which is thrown over his back, the legs hanging down behind the Dog's body. A portion of the Sculpture is broken away. I am not aware of any Sculptures of British Dogs having been found elsewhere, and our ideas of the ancient Hound are derived from drawings on vases and from fragments of ancient pottery. Thus in plate xxviii. of ARTIS's Durobrivæ, we have a representation of Hounds hunting Deer, taken from a piece of Roman pottery discovered near Waternewton, Nov., 1827.[1] The Hounds there represented are similar in figure to our modern breed of Greyhounds, and they appear to have collars round their necks. In the same work, plate liv., is a design of Greyhounds coursing a Hare, the Hounds being similar to those above mentioned, excepting that their tails are not so fine and tapering. These examples probably fairly represent the kind of Hounds used in the chase of the Stag and Hare in this Island by the Romans.

Dr. MUSGRAVE, in his Belgium Britannicum,[2] has touched upon the subject of British Dogs and cites authorities to shew the high estimation in which they were held.

"Divisa Britannia mittit veloces, nostrique orbis venantibus aptos."

Some lines of OPPIAN, and also of CLAUDIAN, describe the British Bulldog, and celebrate his strength and courage; while from STRABO we learn the use made of the Dog in the time of War by the Celtic Tribes. In the course of the late excavations at Uriocouium (Wroxeter) among the quantity of bones found in the ruins, skulls of Dogs have been discovered, which are very similar in shape to that of the animal represented in the Bas-relief found in Walcot.

[1] The Durobrivæ of Antoninus, by E. T. Artis, F.S.A., F.G.S., London, 1828.
[2] Cap. xiii., sec. vi.

TABULA HONESTÆ MISSIONIS,

A GRANT OF ROMAN CITIZENSHIP FOUND IN BATH, Dec. 7, 1815.

AN account of this is given in Archæologia.[1] It was found at Walcot, together with great quantities of Roman Pottery, and came into the possession of Mr. JOHN CRANCH, but is not mentioned in the Catalogue of Roman Antiquities handed over by him to the Corporation of Bath, A.D. 1815. Mr. HUNTER, in the Literary Institution Calendar, mentions it as in the possession of Mr. JOSEPH BARRATT, and it is stated to have been purchased subsequently by Mr. LILLY, Bookseller, Fleet Street, London. Mr. LYSONS communicated to the Society of Antiquaries a Facsimile of the Inscription, which appears to have been imperfect, but to have extended over both sides of the Tablet, and he observes that in form the letters nearly resembled those on Tablets found at Malpas and Sydenham, which contain decrees of the Emperor TRAJAN, and are now deposited in the British Museum.[2] It is probable that the fragment found in BATH contained a decree of the same Emperor or of his successor.

The formal part of the decree, of which enough remains to restore the reading of the whole, differs a little from those of TRAJAN, and contains the words "dimissis honestâ missione," which are those wanting in the Tabulæ above mentioned. After enumerating the several cohorts, &c., it appears to have run thus:—"Qui sunt in Britannia sub o . . . . quinque et viginti pluribusve stipendiis emeritis, dimissis honesta missione; quorum nomina subscripta sunt, ipsis liberis, posterisque eorum, civitatem dedit, et connubium cum uxoribus quas tunc habuissent cum est civitas iis data, aut si qui cælibes essent, cum iis quas postea duxissent, dumtaxat singuli singulas."

[1] Vol. xviii., p. 136, app.
[2] See Mon. Hist. Brit., p. cvi. Lysons's Rel. Brit. Rom., vol. i., p. iv.

For an account of these Tabulæ Honestæ Missionis, or Grants of Citizenship, inscribed on plates of copper, I must refer to Mr. WRIGHT's Celt, Roman and Saxon, p. 362, and to the Rev. J. M'CAUL's Brit. Rom. Inscrip., p. 5. Of the three which are given in the Mon. Hist. Brit., pp. cv., cvi., two are of the time of TRAJAN and one of HADRIAN. Their dates are A.D. 104, 105-6, and 124.

It appears that these Grants of Citizenship were duly registered at Rome, and copies inscribed on plates of copper or bronze were sent to the place where the new citizens resided. The original decree at Rome gave a list of all those to whom the privilege had been granted, but in each copy made for an individual his own name only was given, with occasionally the mention of his wife and children. The names also of attesting witnesses are added.[1]

[1] See M'Caul's B. R. Insc.; also authorities quoted by him: Marini, Atti de Frat. Arv. ii., p. 433. Platamone, Juris Rom., Testimoniis, &c. Morcelli, de Stil. ii., p. 309. Borghesi Acta. Acad. Pont Archæol. x, p. 131. Cardinali, Diplomi Imperiali. Arneth, Zwölf Rœmische Militar-diplome; and Henzen Rhein Jahrbb. xiii., p. 98.

ROMAN ALTARS FOUND IN BATH.

AMONG the most interesting remains of the Roman Period that have been dug up within the City are the Altars bearing Inscriptions to the local divinity or other deities worshipped at that time, and those erected in honour of the reigning Emperor. The character of these Altars is generally plain, consisting of an upright squared pillar from 3 to 4 feet high, with a base and capital, on the top of which is the focus to receive the offering, and at each side of it a roll or scroll. In all the inscribed Altars found in BATH, the sides are plain surfaces, whereas Altars found in other localities are either adorned with figures of the sacrificial instruments, or have the head of the victim or the figure of some animal in relief. The only sculptured Altar found in BATH is that bearing the figures of Jupiter and Hercules Bibax on two sides. The Inscription most prevalent is that to the Goddess SUL or SUL MINERVA, to whom four Altars have been found dedicated, and in one instance the *Numina Augustorum*, or divinity of the reigning Emperors, is united with that of the goddess Sul Minerva.

One Altar is dedicated by a citizen of Trèves, to the divinities of his own land, Mars Leucetius and Nemetona, who were the objects of his peculiar worship, and retained their hold upon his affections, although he was in a land supposed to be under the tutelary care of a different divinity.

Some of these Altars indicate ardent hope or grateful thanks for recovery of health. Thus two Freedmen dedicated Altars to the presiding divinity, for the safety and health of their master, an officer of the 6th Legion, who had probably come to AQUÆ SOLIS for the benefit of its healing Springs ; and an officer of the Second Legion erected an Altar to the Local deity, (uniting the divinity of the Emperors with it),—for himself and those belonging to him. The Sylphs, or divinities presiding over rivers, fountains, hills, villages, &c., have an Altar dedicated to their honour, and in the neighbourhood of BATH one has been found dedicated to Apollo and Hercules, which goes far to establish the fact of the worship of the former in this locality. These Altars have escaped destruction, probably from being buried when the Romans left the Island, or from having been thrown down and left under a mass of other ruins. They were thus preserved from violence in the early ages of Christianity, when such remains were considered especially worthy of destruction. What in those times might justly have created alarm and suspicion, now happily only serves as a record of past ignorance and superstition, and tells of the wonderful change which has been effected in the minds of men by the diffusion of Christian Truth.

ALTAR TO JUPITER AND HERCULES BIBAX.

Nine Altars have been found in BATH since the middle of the last century, or A.D. 1753. One of them only is uninscribed, but two of its sides are sculptured, and the other two are left plain. The subject on the one side is Hercules Bibax, or *Convivial Hercules*, with his Club in his left hand, and a Cyphus, or drinking cup, in his right. The other side bears a figure of Jupiter, with the Eagle at his foot, and the forked Thunderbolt in his right hand.

It seems to have anciently stood in the angle of a Temple, and at present is placed in a similar position in the Vestibule of the Literary and Scientific Institution.

This Altar may have been erected between A.D. 284 and 304, in honour of DIOCLESIAN and MAXIMIAN, the former of whom affected the name and character of *Jupiter*; the latter that of *Hercules*.

An Inscription to DIOCLESIAN and MAXIMIAN, under the titles of Jupiter and Hercules, was found on a column at Clunia, in Hispania Tarraconensis. It is preserved in BARONIUS, OCCO, and GRUTER, p. 280, No. 3 ; with another, No. 4—

DIOCLETIANVS JOVIVS ET
MAXIMIAN HERCVLEVS
CÆS. AVG.
AMPLIFICATO PER ORIENTEM ET OCCIDENTEM
IMP. ROM.
ET
NOM CHRISTIANORVM
DELETO QUI
REMP. EVER
TEBANT.

This Inscription, and another to DIOCLESIAN and GALERIUS, commemorate the terrible persecutions of the Christians under those Emperors. If, in consequence of the apparent eradication of Christianity, the Emperors DIOCLESIAN and MAXIMIAN assumed the titles of Jove and Hercules, then this Altar at BATH, which probably depicts them under those characters, may mark the carrying out of their decrees against Christianity in this City.

PLATE X.
ALTAR TO JUPITER AND HERCULES BIBAX.

PLATE XI.
ALTAR IN THE BUTTRESS OF THE PARISH CHURCH OF COMPTON DANDO, WITH THE FIGURES OF HERCVLES AND APOLLO.

ALTAR IN THE BUTTRESS OF THE PARISH CHURCH OF COMPTON-DANDO; WITH THE FIGURES OF HERCULES AND APOLLO.

A Roman Altar has been built into the North buttress at the Eastern end of Compton Dando Church, about seven miles from BATH.¹ This Altar, which is sadly defaced, owing to the rough treatment it has received, bears two figures, one only just traceable, probably representing Hercules; the other, Apollo playing on his Lyre, is more distinct. Apollo and Hercules seem to be here united on the same Altar, the latter being represented as carrying either a Club or a Cornucopia. Through the courtesy of the Rector and Churchwardens of Compton Dando, I was permitted some years ago to have the Altar taken out of its place; but on examining the back, to see if any Inscription existed, it was found to be perfectly plain. The discovery of this Altar, however, establishes the fact of the worship of Apollo in the neighbourhood of BATH, if not in BATH itself, and for that reason it is here introduced.²

¹ See Drawing on opposite Page.

² I am inclined to think that previously to the extension of Christianity in Britain, and the building of a Church at Compton Dando, a small Temple or Shrine had existed in the pretty secluded valley where the Church now stands. Roman Altars have not unfrequently been found buried in Christian churchyards. Thus at Brignal Old Church (now pulled down and left as a ruin), which is situated in a most picturesque dell, about a mile up the River Greta, above Greta Bridge, Yorkshire, an Altar, on which the name of MARS was just discernable, was found buried in the churchyard. I have a sketch of the Altar, which appears to have been removed. Greta Bridge is represented by Horsley, on somewhat doubtful authority, to have been the Roman station of Magiovæ, and the walls of the fort are very distinct just outside the gate of Rokeby Park. See also, Whitaker's Hist. of Richmondshire, vol. i., p. 148.

ALTAR TO THE LEUCETIAN MARS AND NEMETONA.

The Altar on the opposite page was discovered, according to Mr. WARNER, in 1754, in the upper part of Stall Street. The Inscription, which has been very inaccurately read, from neglect of a close inspection of the stone, is as follows :—

PEREGRINVS
SECVNDI FIL
CIVIS TREVER
LOVCETIO
MARTI ET
NEMETONA
V. S. L. M.

Until lately the word in the fourth line has been read IOVCETIO,[1] and translated to "Jupiter Cetius," or the Cetian Jupiter ; whereas the true reading is LOVCETIO MARTI, i.e., to the Leucetian Mars, ET NEMETONA, and Nemetona. This corrected reading is confirmed by reference to GRUTER, lviii., 3 ; and in STEINER, 1 Dan. et Rh. 1, n. 472, we have

CVRTELIA PREPVSA
MARTI LOVCETIO
V. S. L. L. M.

and

MARTI LEVCETIO
T. TACITVS CENSORINVS
V. S. L. L. M.

The same deities are joined in the following Inscription found at Altripp, *prope Nemetas*, and given by HENZEN, n. 5904 :—

MARTI ET NEMETO
NAE
SILVIN JVSTVS
ET DVBITATVS
V. S. L. L. P.

[1] Lysons, in Reliq. Rom., part ii , plate xi., and p. 10, says in a note—" It seems very uncertain who this *Jupiter Cetius* was," and he endeavours to support this explanation by reference to Muratori, p. viii., 3; p ix., 1 ; and Horsley, p. 278 . IOV. CASIO, and DEO CEATIO. Neither of these explanations, however, is satisfactory.

PLATE XII.
ALTAR TO THE LOUCETIAN MARS AND NEMETONA

For the correct reading of the BATH Inscription we are indebted to the Rev. JOHN McCAUL, LL.D., president of University College, Toronto, who, in a paper read before the Canadian Institute, 30th January, 1857, proposed the emendation, which a careful examination of the stone justifies and confirms. Leucetius, he says, seems to be derived from Leuci, and Nemetona from Nomotes, both being names of peoples in the neighbourhood of the Treviri.[1] Jupiter was also called *Leucetius* as the giver of Light.[2] The meaning of CIVIS TREVER is not a citizen of Troves, but a Trever citizen, *i.e.*, a citizen of the people called Treveri, or Treviri, while it is quite unnecessary to suppose that PEREGRINUS is merely an appellative, as is asserted by Mr. WARNER in his reading of this inscription.[3] The stone may therefore be read as follows:—

"PEREGRINUS the son of SECUNDUS, a Trever citizen, to the Leucotian Mars and Nemetona pays his vows willingly and deservedly."

The height of the stone is 2 ft. 7½ in.

[1] The letter L is so plain in the Inscription, that it would be a matter of wonder how it could have been read as an I, were it not for the known proneness of those who have conceived an interpretation, to wrest the true reading to their own view of what it should be. It is instructive to see with what confidence Mr. Warner adopts the reading, IOVCETIO. (See Illustrations of Rom. Antiq., by the Rev. R. Warner, Bath, 1797.)
[2] See Aul. Gell. Noct. Att., v. 12. Festus s., L.; and Servius on Virgil, Æn. s., 570.
[3] See Illustrations of Rom. Antiq., p. 11.

ON THE DIVINITY SUL AND SUL-MINERVA.

THE Altars dedicated to *Sul*, *Sul-Minerva*, and the *Sulevæ*, are five in number, viz, two dedicated to *Sul*, two to *Sul-Minerva*, and one to the *Sulevæ*; but before entering upon the subject of the inscriptions it will be well to say something of the deity to whom the altars were erected, more especially as the writer of the Historical Ethnology of Great Britain, in the Crania Britannica,[1] has lately been at great pains in the endeavour to elucidate this subject.

From the Altars discovered in BATH, it appears that *Sul* and *Sul-Minerva* were names for the same deity; and a fragment of an Inscription still preserved in the Literary and Scientific Institution would seem to indicate the former existence of a Temple dedicated to this worship.[2] *Sul* seems to have been the divinity presiding over the waters: Apollo was worshiped under this title in Brittany, and after the preaching of Christianity, the name was preserved by its appropriation to a tutelar saint *Sul*.[3]

The worship of the deity *Sul* appears to have been conducted on the tops of hills. Thus, near BATH, we have the isolated hill called *Sol*isbury; and again, *Sal*isbury crags, near Edinburgh, where on the 1st of May (Beltoine), the people assemble to see the sun rise. At Silbury Hill (Avebury), and on other hills in England, a feast is held on Palm Sunday; and of Pontesford, Salop, Mr. HARTSHORNE writes,[4] "A wake is annually held on Palm Sunday on the top of 'Ponsert Hill,' as it is termed, under the pretence of 'socking for the *Golden arrow*.' " For an elucidation of this custom, Mr. HARTSHORNE says he has " in vain looked," but we may venture to suppose that the *Golden arrow* sought for was the benign influence of the sun's rays; that this influence was supposed to be attained by propitiating the *Sun god*, on a certain day; and that the worship of Apollo gave rise to this tradition

[1] See Crania Brit., chap. v., where much learning has been brought together on this difficult subject.
[2] See Rem. Rom. at Bath, in Journal of Brit. Arch. Assoc., December, 1857, p. 279.
[3] See Mém. de l'Acad. Celtique, 1802, tom. iii., p. 311. Sur l'Origine du Culte de St. Sul.
[4] Salopia Antiqua, p. 179.

If this subject were further investigated, it would probably be found that this *cultus* prevailed very extensively in this country in ancient times. CÆSAR says, that the attribute of the Celtic Apollo was the cure and prevention of disease, "Apollinem morbos depellere." Conical rocks and hills were sacred to Apollo, and these, after the introduction of Christianity, were dedicated to St. Michael.

We have in Somerset, Glastonbury Tor with the tower on it, and the dedication to St. Michael preserved in the sculpture still existing there on the chapel; also Montacute. On the coast of Cornwall, we have St. Michael's Mount, and the same on the coast of Brittany, where also is *Tombeleine*, near Avranches, the name being probably derived from Belus or Baal, whose title Baalsemen, Lord of Heaven, is supposed to have been brought to the west by the Phœnicians. In the City of BATH were formerly two churches dedicated to the archangel Michael; one, St. Michael's "intra muros," which has been destroyed, and the site almost forgotten; and the other, St. Michael's "extra muros," which still exists, having been rebuilt within the last thirty years. Dr. THURNAM supposes the church of St. Michael, "intra muros," to have superseded the Temple of Apollo; while the Temple of Minerva was succeeded by the church of St. Mary de Stall, now also destroyed and the site built upon. From SOLINUS we know that *Minerva* was the deity presiding over the mineral waters; and the dedication of two Altars to *Sul-Minerva*, as well as the inscriptions already mentioned, confirm the statement.

The beautiful bronze Head found in Stall Street,[1] *i.e.*, in the street where the church of St. Mary de Stall stood, has given rise to a debate, whether it be a head of Minerva or Apollo. WARNER, in his History of Bath, calls it the latter; HUNTER, in his arrangement of the Catalogue of Roman Remains, considers it to be the former. It is an interesting coincidence, that the form of the face strikingly resembles a terra cotta head of *Pallas Athene*, engraved in BIRCH's Ancient Pottery and Porcelain.[2]

The epithet *Sul* is thought to have had *both* a feminine and masculine application. The Celts had not only a great male divinity, representing the sun, but also a female one, symbolizing the passive powers of nature, by whom the moon was originally intended. This female deity is by CÆSAR identified with *Minerva*. Like the Athene of the Greeks, she was a warlike deity, and venerated by the Britons under the name of ANDRASTE, or ANDATE.[3] ANDRASTE is probably the same as ASTARTE, and only another form of the word. DEA ANDARTE of the Vocontii (Orelli, 1958), is probably the same as the

[1] See p. 25 supra.
[2] Vol. I. p. 194.
[3] See Dion. apud Xiph., lib. 62, vi., vii.

ANDRASTE of Dion. Astarte or Ishtar was, by the Babylonians, known as Queen of Victory.[1]

The remains of a Temple to Luna, or Diana, are preserved in the Literary and Scientific Institution.

To sum up, therefore, before we consider the inscriptions in detail, we have positive proof of the worship of the goddess *Minerva* as Sul-Minerva, the presiding deity of the mineral waters; and we have reason to think that Apollo was also here worshipped, as appears from the altar dedicated to him, now in Compton Dando Church.

[1] See Rawlinson's Herodotus, vol I, Essay x. Altars dedicated to Astarté have been found in Britain. (See Bruce's Rom. Wall, p. 313) Astarté was worshipped under the name Baal בעל the Hebrew, is masculine; but in the lxx., Baal has sometimes the masculine, sometimes the feminine article. Cf. Num xxii., 41; 1 Kings xvi., 31; 1 Sam vii., 4; Hos ii., 8; Tob. 1, 5.

PLATE XIII.
ALTAR ERECTED TO THE GODDESS SUL-MINERVA, BY SULINUS THE SON OF MATURUS.

ALTAR ERECTED TO THE GODDESS SUL-MINERVA, BY SULINUS, THE SON OF MATURUS.

This Altar is a small one, of very elegant form, bearing the following Inscription :—

DEAE
SVLIMI
NERVAE
SVLINVS
MATV
RI. FIL
V. S. L. M.

It was dug up A.D. 1774, by the workmen engaged in removing the rubbish from the head of the spring of the hot bath, near what is now the site of St. John's Hospital, where it had been originally set up, in honour of the tutelary deity of the spring, at the very source,—SULINUS, the son of MATURUS, paying his vow to the goddess of health, Sul-Minerva. Mr. WARNER[1] has a long dissertation on the custom of erecting Altars and making offerings at fountains, and he explains and illustrates the worship paid to them by reference to many classical authorities. At the time the Altar was dug up, many Coins, chiefly of middle brass, were found, extending from NERO to the ANTONINES. The Inscription is read without difficulty, and is very carefully engraved by Mr. LYSONS.[2]

Dr. McCAUL remarks, in reference to it, that "it may be reasonably inferred from the etymology of the name *Sulinus*, and from the circumstance that the individual had but one name, that the dedicator was a barbarian, *i.e.*, a native of Britain or Gaul. This inference, derives support from the order of the words SVLI MINERVAE. If the dedicator had been a Roman, or a Romanized provincial, he would probably have conformed to the usage of placing the designation of the Roman deity first, and that of the identified barbarian deity second. There are many examples of this usage. Among the most obvious are Marti Camulo, Apollini Toutiorigi, Diana Abnoba."

[1] Illustrations of Bath Roman Antiquities ("Altars"), No. III., p. 15 et seq.
[2] Reliquiæ Rom., Part II., pl. n., fig. 1.

ALTAR TO THE DEA SUL-MINERVA ET NUMINA AUGUSTORUM,
ERECTED BY CURIATIUS SATURNINUS.

The Altar on the opposite page, of which the Inscription is—
DEAE SV
LIMIN . ET NV
MIN . AVGG C
CVRIATIVS
SATVRNINVS
... LEG II AVG
PRO SE SV
IS QVE
V S L M.

is engraved in Mr. LYSONS's work, but not in Mr. WARNER's Illustrations. It was found A.D. 1809, some time after the date of the latter publication, when it was discovered in the cistern of the Cross Bath. It is the second Altar dedicated to *Sul-Minerva*, with the NVMINA AVGVSTORVM,—the divinity of the Emperors added,—by C . CVRIATIVS SATVRNINVS, most probably a conturion of the Second Legion, surnamed AVGVSTA, (for the centurial mark which probably occupied the space at the beginning of the sixth line is obliterated) and was erected PRO SE SVIS QVE. The top of the Altar is very perfect. The focus and the ornaments on each side are well marked, but the Inscription is not well preserved. It is a valuable addition to those recorded by Mr. WARNER, and is a further evidence of the worship of the goddess Sul-Minerva. The height of this Altar is 3 feet 8½ inches ; the width, at the capital, 1 foot 6 inches.

PLATE XIV.
ALTAR TO THE DEA SUL-MINERVA ET NUMINA AUGUSTORUM,
ERECTED BY C. CURIATIUS SATURNINUS

PLATE XV.
ALTAR ERECTED TO THE GODDESS SUL BY MARCUS AUFIDIUS LEMNUS,
FOR THE HEALTH AND SAFETY OF AUFIDIUS MAXIMUS.

ALTAR ERECTED TO THE GODDESS SUL
BY MARCUS AUFIDIUS LEMNUS
FOR THE HEALTH AND SAFETY OF AUFIDIUS MAXIMUS.

[D]EAE¹ SVLI
[PR]O SALVTE ET
[IN]COLVMITATE
AV[F]IDI MAXIMI
...LEG. VI. VIC. M.
[A]VFIDIVS LEMNVS
[L]IBERTVS V S L M.

The above Inscription is to the goddess Sul, without the addition of Minerva. It was found, A.D. 1792, on the site of the present Pump Room, where the remains of the temple were discovered, and, therefore, probably stood within the temple. Both Mr. LYSONS and Mr. WARNER have given an engraving of this Altar; but the latter reads the Inscription incorrectly, making the word SVLI at the end of the first line SVLIN, whereas there is no (N) on the Altar itself. This can be clearly ascertained, though the first line of the Inscription is much defaced. The side of the Altar is also broken away, leaving the first two letters of the word PRO and the IN in INCOLVMITATE to be supplied. The stone is also broken before the word LEG, and there is only a slight indication of the centurial mark, noting the rank of AVFIDIVS MAXIMVS, for whose SALVS ET INCOLVMITAS his freedman, M. AVFIDIVS LEMNVS, dedicates this Altar and pays his vows.

¹ The letters in brackets are broken away on the stone.

ALTAR DEDICATED TO THE GODDESS SUL, FOR THE HEALTH AND SAFETY OF AUFIDIUS MAXIMUS, BY HIS FREEDMAN AUFIDIUS EUTUCHES.

Another Altar—

[DEAE] SVLI
[PR]O SALVTE ET
[I]NCOLVMITA
[TE] MAR AVFID
[MA]XIMI > LEG
VI VIC
[A]VFIDIVS EV
TVCH[E]S LEB
V S L M.

The Inscription on this Altar is very similar to the last. It is to the divinity Sul, and for the health and safety of the same individual, only with the addition of the prenomen MARCVS, and a dedication by another freedman, AVFIDIVS EVTVCHES. There is an error in the cutting of the Inscription, LEB being put for LIB. This Altar is much broken at the upper part and cracked across; a portion is also chipped off the side. It is faithfully represented by LYSONS, but incorrectly by WARNER, who reads it, as in the last mentioned Altar, DEÆ SVLINI, whereas it is DEÆ SVLI : he also omits the centurial mark > which is given by LYSONS, and taking the name EVTVCHES to be the words EJVS ADOPTATVS HERES, he supposes the freedman who erected the former Altar to have erected this also. The one, however, was erected by LEMNVS, the other by EVTVCHES, both being freedmen probably of the same master.

The Altars were found together, and may have been set up at the same time in the same Temple. In both these Inscriptions the freedmen appear to have taken the name of their master : each is named AVFIDIVS, each dedicates his offering PRO SALVTE ET INCOLVMITATE, and these Votive Altars remain amid the ruins of the Temple in which they had probably been set up, as testimonies of gratitude for manumission.

PLATE XVI.
ALTAR DEDICATED TO THE GODDESS SUL FOR THE HEALTH AND SAFETY OF AUFIDIUS MAXIMUS BY HIS FREEDMAN AUFIDIUS EUTUCHES.

It is curious, that among the old sculptures described by LELAND as built into the City wall (drawings of which are elsewhere¹ given), there was one which he supposed to be a Roman threatening a Briton; but, if we may trust the drawing given in GUIDOTT's work,² and which has been copied in the present volume, we should rather consider it to represent a Roman who has just placed the cap of liberty on the head of a slave, who is departing from his presence a freedman. This may have been a sculpture representing the manumission of one of the slaves of M. AVF. MAXIMVS, whose health and safety are invoked in the erection and dedication of these Altars.

¹ See pl. L., opposite p 11.
² On the City of Bath and its Bathes. 12mo., Lond., 1669.

ALTAR TO THE SULEVÆ ERECTED BY SVLINUS THE CARVER

An Altar with the Inscription

      SVLEVIS
      SVLINVS
       SCVLTOR
      BRV[C]ETI . F
      SACRVM . F . L . M .

was found, A.D. 1754, or, as Mr. HUNTER says, 1753, at the lower end of Stall Street. It has been engraved in Mr. LYSONS's work and in Mr. WARNER's. It is low in height, broad, and has an oblong hollow at the top to contain offerings of fruits and flowers, or to hold a pan for containing fire.

The last three lines of this Inscription are in letters much smaller and not so deeply cut as the first two lines. Mr. HUNTER thinks that the first two lines are the original Inscription, and the others have been since added, but this is uncertain, for as Dr. McCAUL remarks, "The Greek or Roman stone-cutters seem to have been so capricious as to the size of the letters or the depth of the cutting in the same Inscription, that we are scarcely warranted in inferring in this case two Inscriptions."

The dedication is to the SVLEVÆ, whom Mr. WARNER considers to be "Deæ campestres," or local rural deities of the country around BATH. Mr. LYSONS, in a note, speaks of an Altar dedicated to SVLEVIS et CAMPESTRIBVS, published by FABRETTI in his work De Aquæductibus, and refers to KEYSLER's Antiq. Septentrionales, p. 421. An Altar was found at Nismes with the following Inscription,—

      SVLIVIÆ IDENNICÆ MINERVÆ VOTVM[1]

—in which Minerva seems to have had an appellative very similar to that attached to her name in BATH.

[1] Muratori, p. liii, 5.

PLATE XVII.
ALTAR TO THE SULEVÆ, ERECTED BY SULINUS THE CARVER.

We naturally attach the word SVLEVAE to some divinities connected with SVL, probably her attendant nymphs. Mr. ROACH SMITH says,[1] "The Sulevæ appear to have been sylphs, the tutelary divinities of rivers, fountains, hills, roads, villages, and other localities, against whom were especially directed, in the fifth and subsequent centuries, the anathemas of Christian councils, missionaries, and princes." To these divinities then, SVLINVS SCVLTOR, *i.e.*, *Sulinus* the *Sculptor*, or Stone-cutter (Scultor being probably not the name, but the designation of SULINUS), the son of BRUCETUS, willingly and deservedly set up an Altar. In the case of the dedicator we have an instance of the name of an individual derived from the presiding deity of the waters; this is also to be remarked on another altar [SVL]INVS MATVRI FIL.[2]

[1] Roman London, p. 36 et seq.
[2] See No. 1 of the Altars dedicated to Sul.

FUNEREAL STONE TO CALPURNIUS RECEPTUS, PRIEST OF THE GODDESS SUL.

We conclude the Inscriptions to the divinity Sul by giving the tombstone of one of her priests found in the Sydney Gardens, in the parish of Bathwick, on the South side of the river Avon, A.D. 1795. It is engraved by both Mr. LYSONS and Mr. WARNER, but the latter reads it incorrectly, putting SVLINI for SVLI. The inscription is as follows :—

D. M
C. CALPVRNIVS
[R]ECEPTVS SACER
DOS DEAE SV
LIS VIX . AN . LXXV
CA[LP]VRNIA TRIFO
SA [THR]EPTE CONJVNX
F. C.

Which is expanded thus by Mr. LYSONS :—"Diis manibus Caius Calpurnius receptus sacerdos Deæ Sulis, vixit annos septuaginta quinque Calpurnia Trifosa Threpte conjunx faciendum curavit."

Mr. HUNTER, in the Bath Institution Catalogue, observes that *receptus* may be an appellation of CALPURNIUS, or it may signify that he was an "admitted" priest of the goddess Sul, but "receptus" was probably his cognomen. Mr. WARNER, in his Illustrations, offers no suggestion about the reading of the inscription, but puts SVLINIS for SVLIS, which is an error. He supposes, however, that CALPVRNIVS was a member of the noble Calpurnian family at Rome, which, according to PLUTARCH, traced its origin from CALPO, son of NUMA POMPILIUS, commemorated by OVID as follows :

"Nam quid memorare necesse est
Ut domus a Calpo nomen Calpurnia ducat ?"

CALPURNIUS AGRICOLA was proprætor in Briton under MARCUS AURELIUS.[1] Dr. McCAUL supposes that his name CALPURNIUS may have been derived, as a libertus, from the

[1] See Capitolinus, quoted in the Mon. Hist. Brit., vol. l., lxv.

PLATE XVIII.
FUNEREAL STONE TO CALPURNIUS RECEPTUS, PRIEST OF THE GODDESS SUL.

nomen gentilitium of his master. An Inscription found at Caer Leon contains the name CALPVRNIVS. The following is the reading given by Mr. LEE:—

IOVI O. M. DOLICHV
I ONIO AEMILIANVS
CALPVRNIVS
RVFILIANVS . . EC
AVGVSTORVM
MONITV.

Dr. McCaul observes that the name of his wife, CALPURNIA TRIFOSA THREPTE, seems to afford evidence that the priest "married a Greek slave, that was born and brought up in his own house. TRIFOSA and THREPTE suggest that she was a Greek, and CALPVRNIA and THREPTE that she had been his slave. TRIFOSA, TRYFOSA, TRIPHOSA, and TRYPHOSA, are all latinized forms of a Greek female name, taken, as Symphorusa, Prepusa, Terpusa, and many others, from the nominative singular of the present participle activo ΤΡΤΦΩΣΑ or τρυφωσα, from the verb τρυφάω, the same name that is found in St. PAUL, Epist. ad Rom., xvi., 12. THREPTE or TREPTE probably stands for θρεπτή, the Greek term corresponding to the Latin *Verna*."

The name SVL entering into these six Inscriptions, and the same word being also found in another, apparently the dedication of a building, gives a lofty idea of the importance of this tutelary divinity. I believe that in no other city of England have the remains of a Temple with a dedicatory Inscription, and so many Altars to the same divinity, as well as the tombstone of a priest of that deity, been found, and no Inscriptions to Sul or Sul-Minerva have been met with on Altars in any other place.

FUNEREAL INSCRIPTIONS, &c.

THE Altars dedicated to the goddess Sul and Sul Minerva, and the funereal Inscription to the priest of that goddess having been considered, I now proceed to other funereal Inscriptions which have been found in BATH. Most of these are still in existence, and preserved in the Literary and Scientific Institution. It will be my endeavour to correct some errors in the readings which have been given, so far as further acquaintance with the subject and more recent discoveries enable me.

FUNEREAL STONE TO RUSONIA AVENNA.

RVSONIAE . AVEN
NAE . C . MEDIOMATR
ANNOR . LVIII . H . S . E
L. VLPIVS . SESTIVS
H . F . C

This Inscription is contained on a flat stone, without border or ornament, of the dimensions of three feet one inch, by one foot five inches. It was discovered in the street called the Borough Walls, in 1803.[1] Mr. LYSONS gives an engraving of it,[2] and the Inscription itself is now in the passage of the Literary and Scientific Institution.

Mr. HUNTER[3] says "it appears to have shown the place of interment of Rusonia Avenna, a *centurion* belonging to the nation of the Mediomatrici (a people of Gaul), who died at the age of fifty-eight years ; Lucius Ulpius Sestius caused it to be erected." He

[1] See "Bath Chronicle," May, 1803.
[2] Rel. Rom., part ii., pl. xiii., 1.
[3] Inst. Catalog.

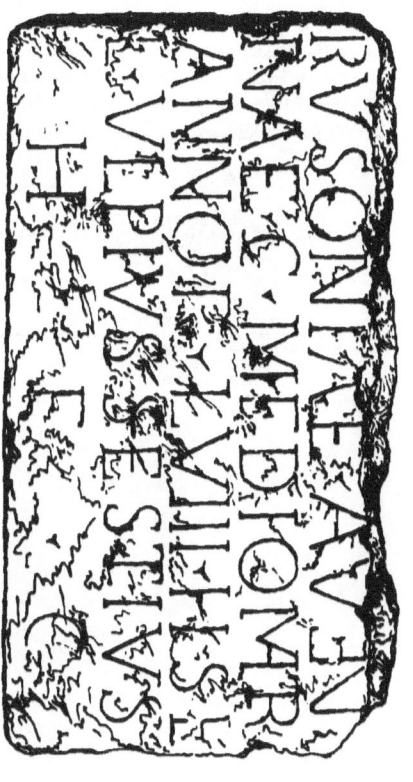

PLATE XIX.
FUNEREAL STONE TO RUSONIA AVENNA.

seems, however, to have been mistaken, not only in the sex of the person to whom the memorial was erected, but also in the meaning of the letter C. The late Mr. LEMAN read it, " To Rusonia Avenna, the wife of Modiomarus."

ORELLI has given an Inscription,[1] found at Mayence, which seems to have been either unknown to, or overlooked by those who have read this Stone. In the Mayence example we have CIVES (sic) MEDIOMATRICA at length, which seems to be the correct reading of the BATH stone ; the C standing for *civis*, not for *centurio* or *conjux*.

We have already recorded an Inscription with CIVIS TREVER, a Trever citizen ; so here we have a citizen of the people called Mediomatrici.[2] These people are mentioned by CÆSAR,[3] as bordering on the Rhine, between that river and the Vosges mountains.[4] Rusonia Avenna was therefore a citizen of that people, who died in BATH, at the age of fifty-eight, and had a stone erected to her memory by L. Ulpius Sestius, her heir.

The Stone is remarkable for the boldness, size, and beauty of the inscribed letters, which are three inches high.

[1] No. 2,523.
[2] The inscription in Orelli is as follows,—see also Gruter, 631, 3—
D. M
PRIMVLAE COMITI.
LAE QVAE VIXIT
ANNIS XX . CIVIS
MEDIOMATRICA
MATERNIVS NEM
AVSVS STRATOR
COS . ET LVCIVS LV
CINVS MENSOR
FRVMENTI NVMER.

The STRATOR CONSULARIS, or consular equerry, here mentioned, was an officer employed to purchase horses for the Roman cavalry. See Rich's Companion to the Greek Lexicon and Latin Dictionary, p. 623.

[3] Bello Gallico, lib iv, 10.
[4] See Strabo, p. 193.

FUNEREAL STONE TO A SOLDIER OF THE XX LEGION.

SER . . . NVS
NIC . EMERITVS . EX
LEG . XX . AN . XLV
H . S . E .
G . TIBERINVS . HERES
F . C.

This funereal stone has been found since Mr. WARNER published his Illustrations in 1797; but it is not known where it was discovered. It is now placed in the passage of the Literary and Scientific Institution. The upper portion of the Inscription has been broken away. Mr. LYSONS, who has given a very correct engraving of it,[1] reads the first letters SER for SERVICE, and supposes the next word to begin with M and end with ONVS; the letters NIC standing for NICON, or probably for NICOMEDIA, the birth place of the deceased.[2] The whole may be read thus :—

SER[GIVS] or SER[VILIVS] [MAG]NVS
NIC[OMEDIA] (the Veteran's birth place)
EMERITVS EX
LEG . XX . AN . XLV
H . S . E
G . TIBERINVS . HERES
F . C .

Whatever may have been the name of the person commemorated, the stone marked the resting place of a discharged soldier of the XX legion, who died at the age of forty-five, and this memorial was erected to him by his heir, GAIVS TIBERINVS. The letters are well cut, and the Inscription is without contractions.

[1] Plate xii., 3.
[2] See an instance of this in an Inscription found in Monmouthshire. (Mr. Lee's Rom. Antiq. found at Caer-Leon, pl. xx., and an explanation of it by Dr. McCaul, Brit. Rom. Insc., p. 111, and note.)

PLATE XX.
FUNEREAL STONE TO A SOLDIER OF THE TWENTIETH LEGION.

PLATE XXIV.
ALTAR ERECTED BY VETTIUS BENIGNUS.

FUNEREAL STONE TO JULIUS VITALIS.

IVLIVS. VITA
LIS. FABRICIES
IS. LEG. XX.V.V.
STIPENDIOR
VM IX. ANNOR. XX
IX NATIONE BE
LGA EX COLEGIO
FABRICE ELATV
S.   IL. S. E.

This interesting monument is now in the passage of the Bath Literary and Scientific Institution. The Inscription, which is well preserved, is contained within a moulding upon an upright stone, having a triangular top, with a device of fruit and flowers. It was found Oct., 1708, on the side of the London Road, Walcot; at the same time a large and a small urn, both containing ashes, were discovered.

The London Road marks the line of the old Foss Way to the village of Batheaston, where it separated into two branches, the one known as the Foss Way leading to Cirencester (Corinium), the other, named the Via Julia, proceeding to Cunetio, near Marlborough.

This Inscription has occupied the attention of many learned men.[1] It is that of a monumental stone, erected to JULIUS VITALIS, a native of Belgic Britain, within which territory BATH was situated. He belonged to the XX legion, V. V. Valeriana, Vitrix, of which he was FABRICIESIS or FABRICIENSIS, *i.e.*, the smith or armourer, and was buried by the company of smiths, as the words EX COLEGIO FABRICE ELATVS lead us to infer; he died in the twenty-ninth year of his age, and the ninth of his service. Mr. WARD says—"It is not improbable this JULIUS VITALIS was a person beloved by his fraternity, who were therefore willing to show so much respect to his memory, and to bury him, and place this stone over him at the common expense."

[1] Musgrave, Dodwell, Hearne (and of Spelman's Alfred), Horsley, Somerset, p. 102. N. 76, p. 323, with some remarks at the end by Ward. Mr. Warner places this inscription the first in his Illustrations; and Mr. Lysons gives an engraving of it, plate xii, 4.

With reference to the word COLLEGIVM, it may be observed that it is found in its proper and usual sense in the famous Sussex Inscription.¹ GALE remarks—"Several sorts of workmen were included under the name FABRI, particularly all those concerned in any kind of building." In later times the FABRI were called FABRICIENSES, and their workhouse was called FABRICA.² Part of the word COLEGIA occurs also in the fragment of the Inscription found on the site of the present Pump Room.³

¹ See Horsley, p. 192, N. 76, also pp. 334-5, for an account of the Collegia.
² For a particular account of the COLLEGIA, see Warner's Illustrations, p. 2.
³ See pp. 19 and 20

FUNEREAL STONES FOUND IN BATH, BUT NOW LOST.

Two sepulchral Inscriptions were found, A.D. 1592, in the line of the old Foss Road, near the place where the Julius Vitalis stone was dug up. They were preserved by Mr. ROBERT CHAMBERS, who thus recorded the discovery on a Stone erected in his garden, near the Cross Bath.

        HÆC . MONVMEN . VIO
        LATA . SVLCIS . IN . CA
        MP . DE . WALCOT . R . C .
        CVLTOR . ANTIQ . HVC .
        TRANSTVLIT . AN
        VER . INCAR . 1592 .

They were seen by CAMDEN, who published an account of them in his Britannia. When GUIDOTT wrote, in 1673, they were in the north wall of a garden, near the Cross Bath, belonging to Mr. CROFTS; HORSLEY saw them in 1725, in a wall attached to the house of Mrs. CHIVES, near the Cross Bath; and in 1749, WOOD says, "they are to be seen in the north wall of the garden which makes Chandos Court incomplete." Since WOOD's time they have disappeared, and have most probably been broken up.

HORSLEY gives a drawing of the first Stone—

        C . MVRRIVS
        C . F . ARNIENSIS
        FORO . IVLI . MO
        DESTVS . MIL
        LEG . II . AD . P . F .
        > IVLI . SECVNDI
        ANN . XXV . STIP . VIII .
        H . S . E .

The latter part of the Inscription was broken away. It commemorated CAIVS MVRRIVS MODESTVS, the son of CAIVS, of the tribe ARNIENSIS,[1] of the town FORO JULII (Friuli), a soldier of the LEG . II . ADJVTRICIS . PIAE . FIDELIS, of the century of JVLIVS SECVNDVS, aged ANN. XXV.[2] The term of his service, STIP . VIII, is

---

[1] Tribus Arniensis, ab Arno, Hetruriae fluvio, erat inter Romanos quinta supra vigesimam. Musgrave, Bel. Brit., cap. vi., § ii., in fine.

[2] See Guidott, p. 86; Musgrave, ii., 7; Horsley Somerset, R.; Wood, II., 429; Gough's Camden, vol. iii., 1; Warner's Ill., introd., p. xxi.

conjectural, as the number was broken out. It appears also from HORSLEY's drawing, that there was space for the centurial mark at the beginning of the sixth line, and therefore it may be supplied. He says that the letters AD . P . F were so distinct in the original, as to leave no room for any suspicion of error, but adds that—" the legio secunda adjutrix, which seems to be here mentioned, was never in Britain, or at least there is no proof of it. The soldier, however, may have come to BATH for his health," or have been a Briton serving in that legion. This seems a more probable conjecture, than to read the Inscription, ADOPTIVVS FILIVS JVLII SECVNDI, which would differ from the common form. According to ordinary usage in Inscriptions, the birth-place follows the cognomen, here it precedes it.¹

Of the second sepulchral Inscription, a drawing is also given in HORSLEY.²

DIS . MANIBUS
M . VALERIVS . M
FIL . LATINVS . ŒQ
MILES . LEG . XX . AN
XXXV . STIPEN . XX
H . S . E .

It commemorates MARCUS VALERIUS LATINUS, the son of MARCUS, a decurion of cavalry, or of the horse which belonged to the XX legion, who died at the age of thirty-five, and in the twentieth year of his service. HORSLEY supposes that " VALERIUS had served in the capacities of a soldier, a horseman, and a decurio equitum in the same legion. Such gradations appear in other Inscriptions."

The only difficulty in the reading is at the end of the third line, where HORSLEY supposing that the tied latter Œ may be either the centurial mark and E, or the letters DE, would read ŒQ as centurio or decurio equitum. It is, probably, D reversed for DECVRIO, and EQ for EQVITVM, for Centurio is only applied to a commander of a body of infantry, and decurio to the commander of a body of cavalry.³ The equites were divided into ten turmæ ; out of each of which three officers were chosen, PRÆFECTI, OPTIONES, DECVRIONES. Dr. McCAUL, however, prefers ORELLI's expansion C[olonia] Eq[uestri], the name of the birthplace of the deceased.

¹ See other examples in Fabretti, pp. 310, 311.
² P. 192, N. 71, and p. 326. See also Camden ; Gaidott, p. 66 ; Musgrave, ii., 6 ; and Warner's Illustrations, introduction, p. xxi.
³ See Polybius, b. vi., p. 171.

FUNERAL STONE TO A DECURION OF GLOUCESTER.

DEC. COLONLÆ GLEV
VIXIT. AN. LXXXVI.

This fragment of an Inscribed Stone, recorded to have been inserted in the city wall, near the North Gate, is now lost.[1] It commemorates a decurion of the colony of Glevum or Gloucester, who died at the age of eighty-six. A decurion was either a senator in any of the municipal towns or colonies, who held a corresponding rank and discharged similar functions in his own town to that which the senators did at Rome, or he was an officer over ten horsemen. In the present instance the individual commemorated seems to have held the former office. ORELLI (99) gives the following Inscription, which may help us to conjecture the part above wanting.[2]

D. M
C. COPONII. CRESCENTIS
DEC. TVSCANENSIVM
QVAEST. R. P. VETER. AVG
LEG XIII. GEMIN. SIGNIFER.
B. M. FECERUNT. C. CAVIVS. PRISCVS. FIL
SCRIBVS. RESTITVTVS. VAL.

[1] It was published by Hearne in his notes to Leland's Itinerary, ii. 35; also by Roger Gale in his Antoninus, p. 129. Gibshal gives it in his Discourse of Bath, p. 69; Musgrave, ii. 1; Horsley's Somerset, v.; Gough's Camden, viii. 3; Warner's Illustrations, introd., p. xiii.

[2] This Inscription corroborates the statement of Richard of Cirencester, that Gloucester was one of the nine Colonia. See Wright's Celt, Roman, and Saxon, p. 389.

PORTIONS OF TWO STONES ERECTED TO ROMAN CAVALRY; THE LATTER BEING THAT OF TANCINUS, A SPANIARD.

L . VITELLIVS . MA
NTAI F. TANCINVS
CIVES. HISP. CAVRIESIS
EQ . ALAE. VETTONVM C R
ANN . XXXXVI . STIP . XXVI
H . S . E .

This Stone, which was found A.D. 1736, in digging a vault in the Market Place,[1] is part of a monument erected to the memory of a horse soldier, who is represented as riding over a prostrate enemy. Similar Stones have been discovered at Cirencester, Gloucester, and Wroxeter. The monument is incomplete, but the upper portion of another monument of a like character supplies what is wanting, though upon a smaller scale. This second stone was, according to Mr. WARNER, found in Grosvenor Gardens.[2]

The stone is broken, and some of the letters in the second and third lines are injured, but the Inscription below the figure is perfect. For many years this stone, together with that erected to IVLIVS VITALIS, were inserted in the wall of the Abbey Church, but both are now placed in the passage of the Literary and Scientific Institution.[3]

The reading is as follows,—

Lucius Vitellius Mantai filius Tancinus cives Hispanus Cauriesis Æques Ale Vettonum, civium Romanorum, ann. xxxxvi. Stip. xxvi. Hic situs est.

Mr. LYSONS reads HISPANLÆ instead of HISPANUS ; EQVITVM instead of EQVES ; and C . R . CENTVRIO instead of CIVIVM ROMANORVM ; but the last two readings are evidently erroneous, and HISPANVS is better than HISPANLÆ. The Rev. Dr. MCCAUL has pointed this out in his Britanno-Roman Inscriptions.[4]

[1] Collinson's Somersetshire, vol. I., p. 12.
[2] See Illustrations, p. 10.
[3] See Muratori, DCCCLXX., 6; Gough's Camden, vol. iii. 8 ; Warner's Illustrations, No. 11. Hist. App. p. 118; Lysons, sil., 1 ; Phil. Trans., 1748.
[4] See p. 184.

PLATE XXIII.
PORTIONS OF TWO STONES ERECTED TO ROMAN CAVALRY, THE LOWER BEING THAT OF TANCINUS, A SPANIARD.

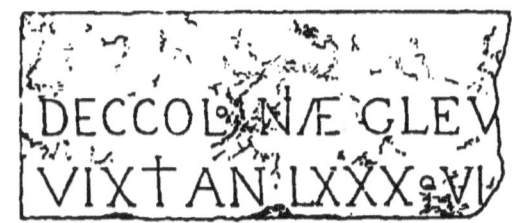

PLATE XXII.
FUNEREAL-STONES FOUND AT BATH, BUT NOW LOST.

The stone was erected to LUCIUS VITELLIUS TANCINUS, the son of MANTAUS, a citizen of Caurium, in Spain, a soldier of the Vettonesian auxiliary cavalry, who died at the age of forty-six, having served twenty-six years. The Vottonesian auxiliary cavalry consisted of men who had obtained the rights and privileges of Roman citizens.

The name TANCINVS occurs in an inscription found in Lusitania.[1] Caurium was a town of Lusitania in the district of Estremadura.[2] The Vettones were a neighbouring people who furnished heavy armed cavalry as auxiliaries to the Roman armies.

The use in this Inscription of long triangular leaves with stalks as stops, would seem to indicate a rather late date; but Dr. CONRAD LEEMANS, of Leyden, in treating of the monumental stones of a like character, found at Watermore, near Cirencester, says,[3] that the Watermore Inscriptions may be fixed between the time of the expedition of AGRICOLA and the reign of AURELIUS and his first successors, and the sepulchral Stones of horsemen of the Roman allies, found at BATH and in Shropshire, may belong to the beginning of the same period.

[1] See Gruter, DCCCCXVII., 8.
[2] See Hoff., Lexicon, tom. I., p. 778.
[3] Archæol., xxvii., p. 211.

INSCRIPTION ON A STONE ERECTED BY VETTIUS BENIGNUS.

The following Inscription is on a Stone, shaped like an Altar, but without any focus.

NA SACRAT[I]
SSIMA VOTV
M SOLVIT
VETTIVS BE
NIGNVS . L . M.

It was found near the Hot Bath, A.D. 1776, and is engraved and described in Lysons's Remains[1] ; but is wrongly given in Collinson's History of Somerset.[2] Mr. Warner, in a note to his Illustrations, reads it

DEAE DIA
NAE SACRATI
SSIMAE . . . . .

but the first words, Deae Dianæ, are an invention. The Inscription really begins thus—

NASACRAT

the first letter being defaced, and only the last portion of it clear. There is, however, a mark which seems to be the slanting stroke of an N, and the letter was probably N and not I with the P before it, as conjectured by Mr. Lysons, who would read it PIA SACRATISSIMA. If the letters NA, in the first line, may be taken as standing for NVMINA AVGVSTI, with the epithet SACRATISSIMA, then the Inscription becomes intelligible, which it was not before.

[1] See p. 11.
[2] Vol. L., p. 14.
[3] See p. 23.

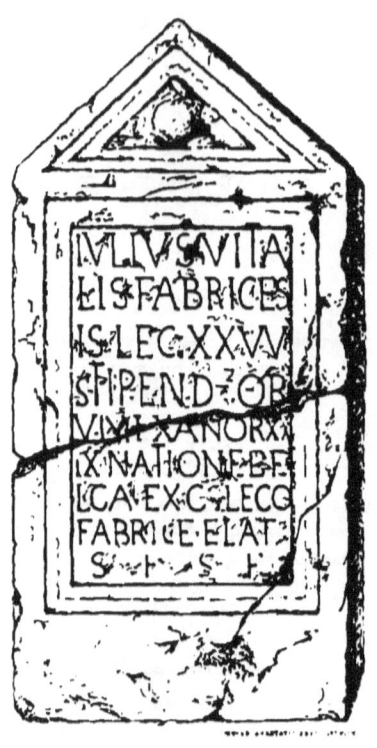

PLATE XXI
FUNEREAL STONE ERECTED TO JULIUS VITALIS

The title Sacratissima was applied to the Numina Augusti; thus in GRUTER' we have

SACRATISSIMO IMP HADRIANO AVG

and also *Sanctissimus, venerandus venerandissimus*²; while on the Altar found at Risingham, Northumberland,³ we have N . D . N, Numini domini nostri.

The first inscription given by GRUTER relates to the dedication of a Statue, and this stone, on which the BATH inscription occurs, seems rather to have been the Pedestal of a Statue, though in the form of an Altar; indeed, the stone, which is perfectly plain, has no focus on the top, and, from being cut away at the back, appears to have been inserted in the wall of a building. We may conjecture, therefore, that VETTIVS BENIGNVS paid his vow by putting up a Statue or other offering in honour of the most sacred divinity of the Emperor. I am aware that authority is wanting for reading N . A, as I have done, the words being generally written NVMIN . AVG, as in the Altar dedicated by CAIUS CURIATIUS SATURNINUS,⁴ or N . AVG, as in the commemorative inscription which follows,⁵ and that in a dedication we should have the dative case, i.e., NVMINIBVS SACRATISSIMIS. I offer, however, the above reading as nearer the truth, and more satisfactory than that of Mr. LYSONS.

¹ ccccxlvi., 4.
² See Gruter, ci., 7; clxv.; cclxxii., 5, 9; cclxxxiii., 9; ccix., 5.
³ See Camden, edit. 1607, p. 683.
⁴ See Lysons, xiii., 2.
⁵ See also Warner, No. IX.

STONE COMMEMORATING THE RESTORATION OF A SACRED SPOT,
OR "LOCUS RELIGIOSUS."

LOCVM RELI
GIOSVM PER IN
SOLENTIAM E
RVTVM
VIRTVTI ET N
AVG REPVRGA
TVM REDDIDIT
C SEVERIVS
EMERITVS)
PEC

This Stone was found at the lower end of Stall Street, A.D. 1753, with two Altars already mentioned ; viz., one to the SVLEVÆ, and the other to the Leucotian Mars.

The Inscription, which is thought by Mr. WARD to be of the age of SEVERUS,[1] is very interesting, as it raises a question—What was this LOCVS RELIGIOSVS ? and—What is implied by PER INSOLENTIAM ERVTVM ? To this, it may be answered,—It was probably a temple or small chapel dedicated to the presiding divinity that had been overthrown in some tumult of party feeling, or left in neglect. The Roman military officer of the locality restored and re-purified it. VIRTUTI ET NVMINI AVGVSTI, to the virtue and deity of AVGVSTUS. The Numen Augusti occurring here strengthens the conjecture as to the correct reading of the last Inscription. The centurial mark) follows the word EMERITVS, which may be either a cognomen or an appellative intimating that C . SEVERIVS had completed his term of service and received his discharge ; probably it was here a cognomen. The last letters may be read PEC, and S, for sua, obliterated. They are of a smaller size, and Mr. HUNTER supposes they may have been scratched on the stone by a wanton hand.

[1] See Phil. Trans., xlviii., 333; Gough's Camden, vol. iii., p. 9; Lysons's Rel. Rom., part ii., p. 10, and note ; also Warner's Ill., No. IX., p 47 ; and Anti-Jacobin Review, x.

PLATE XXV.
ALTAR ERECTED TO COMMEMORATE THE RESTORATION OF A "LOCUS RELIGIOSUS."

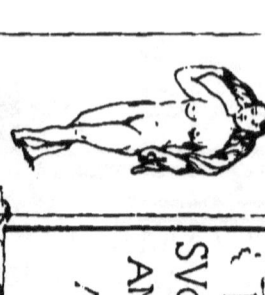

D M
SVCC PETRONIAE VIX
ANI · II I · M · IIII D · IX V · PO
MVLVS · FICTSARINA
FIL · KAR · FEC ·

PLATE XXVI.
FUNEREAL STONE TO SUCCIA PETRONIA.

The worship of the Roman Emperors living and dead was a peculiarity of the later system of Roman religion. Under the title of "Augustus" men's minds were directed to something superhuman.[1] In after times the Emperor was to be worshipped as a Deity present in the body: "Tanquam præsenti et corporali deo fidelis est præstanda devotio." The provinces contended against one another in dedicating Temples and Altars to the living and dead Augustus. By the time of Tiberius it had become a crime to testify indisposition to worship the imperial god, and for it the city of Cyzicus forfeited its freedom.[2]

It was a principle in Rome till the time of Caius Caligula to follow the general analogy of the Manes, and not to raise the Cæsar to divine honours till after his death, and then by special decree of the senate and his successor. Caius desired to be acknowledged and worshiped throughout the whole Empire equally as a visible god while living.

Afterwards Princesses of the imperial family came to be deified. Caius had the same divine honours as were paid to Augustus decreed to his sister, Drusilla. Claudius raised his grandmother, Livia, to the same dignity. Nero had his father, Domitius, and Poppæa, his wife, exalted into deities.

Domitian stiled himself in documents "lord and god." The roads to the Capitol, Pliny tells us, were filled with flocks and herds, that were being driven to be sacrificed before his image.[4]

The greatest extravagance on this head was reserved for Hadrian's time. Between the first deification of Cæsar and the apotheosis of Diocletian, fifty-three solemn canonizations may be reckoned, fifteen of which were of ladies belonging to the imperial family.[5]

[1] Dio Cassius.
[2] Lydus de mens. iv., 72; Vegetius 25.
[3] Tac. Ann., iv., 36.
[4] Sust. Dom., 13; Oros, vii., 10; Plin. Paneg., 11.
[5] Abridged from Döllinger's Gentile and Jew, vol. II., pp. 165, 166, 167, 168, 169.

FUNEREAL INSCRIPTION TO SUCCESSA PETRONIA.

D.   M.
SVCC. PETRONIAE VIX
ANN III . M . IIII . D . IX . VERO
MVLVS ET VICTISARINA
FIL . KAR . FEC.

The Stone which bore this Inscription is now lost ; it is recorded to have been inserted in the city wall, between the North and West Gates, whither it had been brought from one of the Roman cemeteries that followed the lines of road out of the city. LELAND[1] who first mentions it, describes it as among the antiquities he saw in the walls between the two gates. Dr. GUIDOTT says—"Next to that lower, towards the West Gate, is the monument of one of the children of two Romans : PRIMVLVS . ROMVLVS VIPOMVLVS, or rather VETEROMVLVS (for that word in the Stone is somewhat difficult to read), and VICTISARINA, with a longer and exactly Roman Inscription in a sepulchre table between two little images, whereof the one holds the horn of Amalthæa or Cornucopia, the other bringeth a flying roll, or winding list or banner over the left shoulder."[2] This Inscription was sent by CAMDEN to GRUTER, and it is given in his Thesaurus, DCC., 6, but the reading differs. HORSLEY also furnishes a drawing of it,[3] and observes that the two figures on each side have nothing to do with the Inscription, but are on different Stones.[4]

Dr. McCAUL[5] proposes to read the Inscription thus :

D[IIS] M[ANIBUS]
SVCC[ESSAE] PETRONIAE
VIX[IT] ANN[IS] III . M[ENSIBVS] IIII . D[IEBVS]IX .
VET[TIVS] ROMVLVS ET VIC[TORIA] SABINA
FIL[IAE] KAR[ISSIMAE] FEC[ERVNT]

[1] Itinerary, vol. ii., 36.
[2] See Guidott's Discourse of Bathe, pp. 69, 70 ; London, 1676. He gives a drawing of it, and reads it as above.
[3] See also Gough's Camden, vol. iii., 4 ; and Warner's Illust., Introd., p. xxii , where the reading differs considerably.
[4] See Horsley's Somerset, iv.
[5] Brit. Rom. Insc., p. 162.

The difficulty is in the father's name, which most probably consisted of two words, as suggested above, and likewise in that of the mother. On the Stones, which, according to HORSLEY, "are three distinct Stones, and do not appear to have been ever united," were two figures which accompanied the Inscription. In the drawing they are represented on either side, and have a strong resemblance to Christian emblems. "One of these," says HORSLEY, "is a Victory with a palm branch in her left hand, and a corona in her right." The other, as Dr. STUKELEY thinks, "has a cornucopia in her loft," though, as he says, "they have no reference to the Inscription near which they are placed."

It might be supposed that the figure to the left of the Inscription was that of the "Good Shepherd," bringing back the wandering sheep, and that the figure to the right was "Victory" with the palm branch. A similar pair is found in MAFFEI's Musæum Veronense; but the good shepherd is usually represented with a tunic and buskins. It is worthy of remark, that the name PETRONIA is met with in Christian Inscriptions, and that VICTORIA and SABINA, as well as SVCCESSA, are found in the catacombs at Rome. There is also a saint Romulus at Velletri, whose body was taken out of the catacomb of St. Cyriac. It is much to be regretted that the originals are lost, and that the copy, both of the Inscription and accompanying Figures, is probably very imperfect. The monument, however, is an interesting memorial of family affection.

FUNEREAL INSCRIPTION TO AN ALUMNA.

D . M.
MERC   MAGNII .
ALVMNA VIXIT AN . I
M . IV . D . XII.

This Funereal Inscription was found, A.D. 1809, near the old North Gate, under Cavanagh's Bank, and was preserved by Mr. BARRATT. It is now in the Literary and Scientific Institution. No engraving of it was given in WARNER's History or Illustrations, as it was discovered subsequently to the publication of those works ; but an excellent engraving is given in Archæologia,[1] and is there described in a letter from the late JOSEPH HUNTER, F.S.A., dated April 9th, 1827. The Inscription is to an " Alumna of Mercurialis or Mercutius Magnius, who died, aged one year, four months, and twelve days." The space between MERC and MAGNII was left blank when the Inscription was cut.

ORELLI has this note upon the word " alumna,"—" Sæpo memorantur ALVMNI et ALUMNAE (θρεπτοι) *i.e.*, liberi nati, expositi, deinde sublati a quibusdam et in servitudine educati."[2]

[1] Vol. xvii., p. 420, appendix.
[2] Trajan, Ep. ad Plin., 10, 72.

PLATE XXVIII.
PART OF AN INSCRIPTION, PUT UP BY THE SON OF NOVANTUS, IN CONSEQUENCE OF A DREAM.

PLATE XXVII.
FUNEREAL STONE TO AN ALUMNA.

PART OF AN INSCRIPTION PUT UP BY THE SON OF NOVANTUS.

NOVANTI FIL
PRO SE ET SVIS
EX VISV POSVIT

This Inscription is on the front of a large block of stone, now in the Literary and Scientific Institution, and was found in 1825, in digging for the foundations of the United Hospital, not far from the place where the Altars were discovered, A.D. 1733. It appears to have formed part of a building, and there were probably two lines, if not more, on the stone above it. It was first described by Mr. Hunter,[1] who says—" It indicates that the son of NOVANTUS erected something, probably a sepulchre, for himself and his family ; on comparing this Inscription with some in GRUTER, I concludo that the full form must have been this : first, the name of some god or goddess ; second, the name of the party ; third, the Inscription, as above exhibited. Thus perhaps :

"[DEAE SVLIMINERVÆ
MARCVS AVFIDIVS MAXIMVS]
NOVANTI FILIVS
PRO SE ET SVIS
EX VISV POSVIT."

" For," he continues, " I observe in GRUTER, that 'ox visu' is used only in reference to something done towards the gods." On this it may be observed that if *Novanti Filius* was a Barbarian, as probably *Secundi fil.* and *Bruceti fil.* were, then like them he would only have one name.

[1] See Archæol., vol. xxii., p. 420, Appendix, in the same letter in which the foregoing Inscription is given.

INSCRIPTION TO VIBIA JUCUNDA.

```
VIBIA
IVCVN
DA
AN. XXX
HIC SEPVL
TA EST.
```

The Inscription, which is read as above in BURTON's Commentary on Antonine, is a brief record of Vibia Jucunda, who died at the age of thirty, and was buried beneath the stone.

PHILIPOT, who wrote A.D. 1660, says, in his "Villare Cantianum," that this Inscription was found not many years before " at the BATH," and "represented to public inspection." He describes it as "an urn with this endorsement insculpted;"[1] but as "an urn" in those days did not necessarily mean a piece of pottery, it is probable that a "sepulchral tablet" was intended.

The Inscription is given by GUIDOTT,[2] who says it was found in Walcot. WARNER has copied what GUIDOTT says, but it was erroneously thought by HORSLEY to be spurious. It was formerly in the possession of Alderman JOHN PARKER.

[1] See Vil. Can., p. 250
[2] See p 72.

INSCRIPTION FOUND AT COMBE DOWN, HAVING BEEN USED AS A COVERING STONE TO A COFFIN OF THE SAME MATERIAL.

```
PR[O] SAL[V]TE IMP . CES . M . AVR
ANTON[I]NI PII FEL[I]CIS INVIC
TI AVG . . . . NAEVIVS AVG
LIB ADIVT PROCC PRINCI
PIA RVINA OPRESS A S[O]L[O] RES
TITVIT
```

This Inscription, which is now in the BATH Literary and Scientific Institution, was found at Combe Down, a village about one mile south of BATH, in 1854. It was discovered while making a garden to a new villa, and served as the covering stone for the lower part of a Stone Coffin, in which was a perfect skeleton. This spot has since proved to have been the site of a Roman villa, and many objects of interest which have been discovered there, are carefully preserved by the owner. Five Stone Coffins have been found on the spot, besides urns containing burnt bones, and a stone box containing the head of a Horse.[1]

The Inscription, which is not deeply cut, is difficult to read, owing to the decomposition of the stone. It is as follows : " For the safety of the Emp. Cæs. MARCUS AURELIUS, ANTONINUS, the pious, fortunate, invincible AUGUSTUS, Nævius Freedman of the Emperor, and assistant of the procurators, restored the chief military quarters which had fallen to ruin."

The word PRINCIPIA, in the fourth line, is only made out with difficulty ; but there seems no doubt of the correctness of the reading, as it is corroborated by a Stone found at Lanchester,[2] where we have

```
PRINCIPIA ET ARMENTARIA
CONLAPSA RESTITVIT.
```

[1] See Somerset Archæological Journal, vol. v., p. 49, and Appendix, p. 133.
[2] See Horsley, Durham, No. XII.

This affords proof of the existence of a class of buildings called PRINCIPIA. "Locus in Castris ubi erat prætorium, et tabernacula legatorum et tribunorum militum, et signa legionum ; et ubi conciones militares et consilia habebantur, jus dicebatur, sacra fiebant, ἀρχεῖα."[1]

There is no evidence that the Principia stood where the Stone was found. Indeed the Stone seems to have been cut and prepared in the quarry near at hand, and then thrown aside, and afterwards used for the purpose of a coffin lid. The site of the Roman building and its enclosure, together with the remains found, do not give the idea of a military station, unless it was a summer residence for the officer in command, at a time of much security. The dedication may refer either to CARACALLA or HELIOGABALUS.

[1] See Facciol., in Verb. Principium.

PLATE XXX.
FRAGMENT OF MARBLE TABLET.
FRAGMENT OF INSCRIPTION ON SANDSTONE.

marble is mentioned by Mr. ROACH SMITH ;[1] and what WHITAKER calls "the square marble urn, which tradition reports to have been found at Rokeby, in Yorkshire," may therefore be genuine, and the tradition respecting it perfectly correct. From this it certainly appears that, notwithstanding WHITAKER'S assertion to the contrary, the Romans did use marble in this country, but probably imported it from the Continent, and its use was not very frequent. This discovery in BATH therefore serves to remove doubt as to other marble Inscriptions said have been found in England, but the authenticity of which has hitherto been disputed.

An Inscribed marble Roman Funereal Tablet was exhibited in the Museum of the Archæol. Institute at Rochester, July, 1863.

FRAGMENT OF AN INSCRIPTION ON SANDSTONE.

CORNELIANV.

The two portions of stone upon which the above Inscription is cut, were always considered as containing parts of two different words, and are given as such by Mr. HUNTER, in his Catalogue;[2] but Mr. RUSSELL, the Librarian of the Institution, on examining the fragments, and placing them together, found that the portions belonged originally to one stone. The letters form the word CORNELIANVS, with apparently the lower portion of the letter (S) preceding them.

Three other lettered fragments have already been mentioned,[3] but they are not sufficiently perfect to enable us to make out any name with certainty, or to hazard any reasonable conjecture as to their meaning. The three fragments[4] are as follow:—

| VRN | LIIVSSA | ILIA |
| IOP | SVXSO | VLIA |

Future excavations may reveal the missing portions, if they are still in existence; at all events, it is important to preserve a record of the letters.

[1] Rom. Lon., p. 29.
[2] See page 77.
[3] See p. 10.

[4] Engraved by Musgrave, cap. vi., tab. ii.; see also, Guidott, p. 62; Hearne in Leland's Itinerary, ii., 36; also Warner's Illustrations, introd., p. xxiii.

FRAGMENT OF AN INSCRIPTION ON MARBLE.

This discovery of an inscribed marble fragment[1] is not one of the least interesting and important to antiquaries. It was made A.D. 1861, on the site of the new building, added to the Bath Mineral Water Hospital, when a tessellated pavement, of a rude description, was laid open, and many Roman coins and much pottery were dug up. These are all preserved in the Literary and Scientific Institution, and an account of them was read to the Somerset Archæological and Natural History Society, at their meeting in August, 1862, and published in their proceedings.[2] The Inscription is on white marble, apparently foreign, since none is found in England, though it is in Ireland.

The letters are as follows :—

    DEAE . S
    TI . CL . T
    SOLLEN

(also portions of letters, which may be E or F, and L I, or I I or II, of smaller size.)

The letters are particularly well cut, and seem to belong to an early period of the Roman occupation of our Island. The small fragment of the letter S leaves little doubt that the dedication was to the DEA SVL or SVLMINERVA to whom, as we have seen, six Inscriptions relate, and also a temple or other building was dedicated. In the second line we have the abbreviations of two names of the dedicator TI(BERIVS) CL(AVDIVS), with a triangular stop after each, clearly cut, and the first letter of the cognomen (T), which may be any Roman name beginning with that letter. The third line commences with the word SOLLEN ; but the remainder is broken away, leaving us to conjecture that it was the word SOLLENNES or SOLEMNES, and referred to the vows paid to the tutelary goddess. The word SOLLEMNIS occurs in an Inscription on marble, preserved in FABRETTI,[3] and also given in ORELLI,[4] and is a fragment of a funereal laudatory Inscription of the AUGUSTAN age. The letters commencing the fourth line are cut smaller, but it is not possible to conjecture the word of which they formed components.

The finding of this Inscription in marble, induces the belief that tablets of marble were not so uncommon in Britain as has been supposed. A Sepulchral Inscription in Purbeck

---

[1] See plate xxx.
[2] See vol. xi., p. 197.
[3] See pp. 168 and 323.
[4] See 4509.

PLATE XXIX.

INSCRIPTION FOUND AT COMBE DOWN, HAVING BEEN USED AS A COVERING STONE TO A COFFIN OF THE SAME MATERIAL.

INSCRIPTION FOUND AT CAMERTON.

AIIVS
ONDEDIT
ET QVINTIANO COS.

The above Inscription was found, not in BATH, but six miles out of BATH, in the parish of Camerton, on the line of the Foss Road, A.D., 1814. It was recorded by Mr. SKINNER, the rector of Camerton, in a letter to the late SAMUEL LYSONS, Esq., F.S.A., and the MS., which appears to have been read to the Society of Antiquaries, is in the possession of the Rev. S. LYSONS, of Hempstead Court, Gloucester. A drawing of the Stone is preserved with the MS. The Inscription is also recorded by Mr. LEMAN, in a marginal manuscript note to his copy of HORSLEY'S Brit. Rom., now in the Library of the BATH Literary and Scientific Institution.

The Inscription, which was on white lias stone, was found in digging out the remains of a building which was one of several that bordered on the line of the Foss Road, six miles from BATH, and about a mile beyond the Red Post Inn. It is not known what has become of it. With it were found part of a stone statue and pieces of painted stucco. The first line is much defaced, only the letters A, V, and S, being distinctly legible. The letters between the A and V may have been a T and I, or P and I, or II, so that the name seems to have terminated in the form ATIVS, or APIVS, or AIIVS. The next word is plainly [C]ONDEDIT, an E being put for an I. In the third line we have ET QVINTIANO COS. So that we are able to supply what is wanting, knowing that BASSUS was consul with QUINTIANUS, A.D. 289, *i.e.*, in the first or second year of CARAUSIUS.[1] The Inscription will therefore stand thus—

Name of person who erected the building, ending ATIVS or APIVS or AIIVS
CONDIDIT
BASSO ET QVINTIANO COS

[1] See Stukeley's *Carausius*, vol. 1, p. 72.

In the fac-simile which Mr. SKINNER has preserved in his MS., the Stone is small, about 8 in. by 2½ in., and the building itself appears not to have been mentioned in the Inscription, only the name of the builder and the date. It was found in digging out the interior of a small inner chamber.[1]

Thus from this fragment we can fix the date of the erection or re-erection of this structure, as from Mr. SKINNER's account it seems to have been built out of the materials, and upon the site of older buildings, which not improbably marked the first posting station out of AQUÆ SOLIS, on the Foss Road towards Ischalis (Ilchester). Many Roman Coins have been discovered at Camerton, chiefly in the field containing the building wherein the Inscription was found. The Coins extend over a period from CLAUDIUS to VALENTINIAN I.

With this Inscription ends the list of those found in BATH and the immediate neighbourhood. The lists hitherto given, even that contained in the catalogue of the BATH Literary and Scientific Institution, are imperfect. It has been my endeavour to bring together as correct an account as possible of each lettered stone, that all may be accurately recorded in the pages of this Volume. That many yet remain to be discovered is my belief, and I am not without hope that some supposed to be lost may yet be recovered.

[1] See Som. Arch. and N. H. Proc., vol. xi., p. 181.

PLATE XXXI.
STONE FOUND IN BATH.

SCULPTURED STONE FOUND IN BATH.

THE Sculpture, of which a plate is given opposite, represents a Roman clad in a loose cloak, apparently fastened over the right shoulder by a fibula, or clasp. The hair of the head is cropped, and the beard is evidently short and curling, though the carving of the face is here broken away. The Stone was found on the Borough Walls, with some remains of Roman masonry, and fragments of a cornice, A.D. 1803, and seems to have been brought from its original situation, and built into the City Wall. Mr. WARNER gives a drawing of it in his Illustrations,[1] and supposes it to be a figure of the Usurper CARAUSIUS, on account of the Dolphin which appears at the right hand upper corner of the Stone. The dolphin, however, was a common ornament on Funereal Monuments, and this figure was probably a portion of some such memorial, the Inscription having been placed under the feet of the figure. Dolphins are represented on the sides of a Funereal Inscription found at Wroxeter, and now in the Library of King EDWARD's School in Shrewsbury.[2]

The treatment of the hair and beard led Mr. WARNER to attribute the Sculpture to the period of the lower Empire, after the Emperor HADRIAN, in the beginning of the second century, had revived the ancient Roman custom of wearing beards, which had long been out of fashion.[3] It is not possible to conjecture either the exact date of this Sculpture, or the person to whom it was erected, but it was probably executed about the third or fourth century of the Christian era. There is no authority for supposing it to be a representation of CARAUSIUS. The figure, if not a portion of a tomb, probably formed part of the decorations of some public edifice. The dress is more like that of a Roman citizen in the toga than of a military officer in the chlamys or sagum.

[1] No. X., p. 49.
[2] See British Archaeol. Journal. 1859, p. 311.
[3] The Romans adopted the Oriental custom of shaving the chin about 300 years after the foundation of the city, and continued it to the time of Hadrian. See Xiphilinus in Vita Trajani.

L

ANOTHER SCULPTURED STONE FOUND IN BATH.

The mutilated fragment, drawn in the plate opposite, represents a Roman Standard-bearer, clad in a tunic, with a belt (cingulum) round the waist, and the chlamys or military cloak over the shoulders. The right hand grasps the staff of a standard, and in the left a scroll is held. The head and neck of the figure are unfortunately broken off, and the feet, as well as the lower part of the stone, are wanting, so that it is difficult to assign any date to the Sculpture, or form a right conjecture as to its object. It was probably, however, a portion of a tomb erected to some Standard-bearer of note. The fragment is now placed in the Vestibule of the Literary and Scientific Institution. It is not engraved in WARNER's Illustrations, nor is it known where it was found.

PLATE XXXII.
STONE FOUND IN BATH.

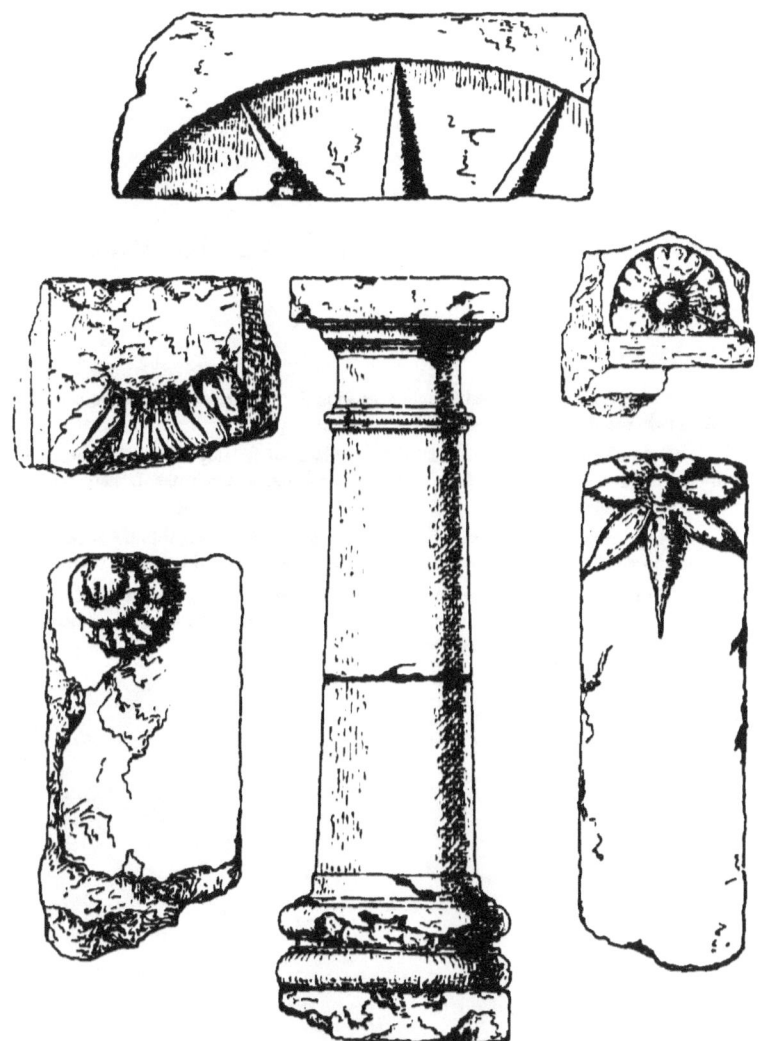

PLATE XXXIII.

ROMAN FRAGMENTS FOUND IN BATH.

Various fragments of Roman Sculpture found in BATH are represented on the plate which faces this page.

In the centre of the plate is a small Column, which has probably supported a statue. It was found when the Roman Baths were uncovered, and is now in the Literary and Scientific Institution.

The remaining fragments were found underneath the Pump Room, with the remains already described,[1] and seem to have formed a portion of the Temple which stood on that site.

The upper fragment contains three rays of a Star, projecting from a concave surface, and there is also a Star with eight rays on the lower oblong block. The three other pieces are ornamental portions of Architectural Details.

[1] See p. 16, et seq. supra.

BRONZE MEDALLION.

THE beautiful Medallion here represented[1] was found in digging the foundation of the Pump Room, a locality where so many other interesting remains have been discovered. It is engraved by Mr. WARNER in his History of BATH,[2] and he considers it to be assignable to a late date in the Empire. This interesting souvenir became the property of the Rev. Mr. RICHARDSON, who presented it to the BATH Literary and Scientific Institution, where it is still preserved.[3] Mr. WHITAKER supposes it to have hung in the Temple of Minerva, on the site of which it was found.

The subject is the head of a female, very beautifully formed, the hair being collected in a knot behind, and the forehead decorated with a pointed frontlet, which is studded with jewels. The frontlet slopes down the forehead to both ears, and after passing under the hair, is fastened by a fillet or band. A pendant lock of hair falls gracefully from behind the ear upon the neck.

The Legend is POMPEIA . I . C . V ., in all probability the name of the lady represented, who is supposed to have been a descendant of POMPEY the Great. Mr. WHITAKER would read the letters I . C . V . JULII CÆSARIS UXOR, because the family of POMPEY afterwards became united by marriage with that of his former rival and competitor for the empire. He also supposes that this Medallion must have been given to the Temple in BATH by some descendant of the family settled in AQUÆ SOLIS.

[1] Plate xxxiv., opposite.
[2] Appendix, p. 183.
[3] Review of Warner's History of Bath ; Antijacobin Review, vol. x.

PLATE XXXIV.
LOCKET FOUND IN BATH, UNDER THE PUMP ROOM.

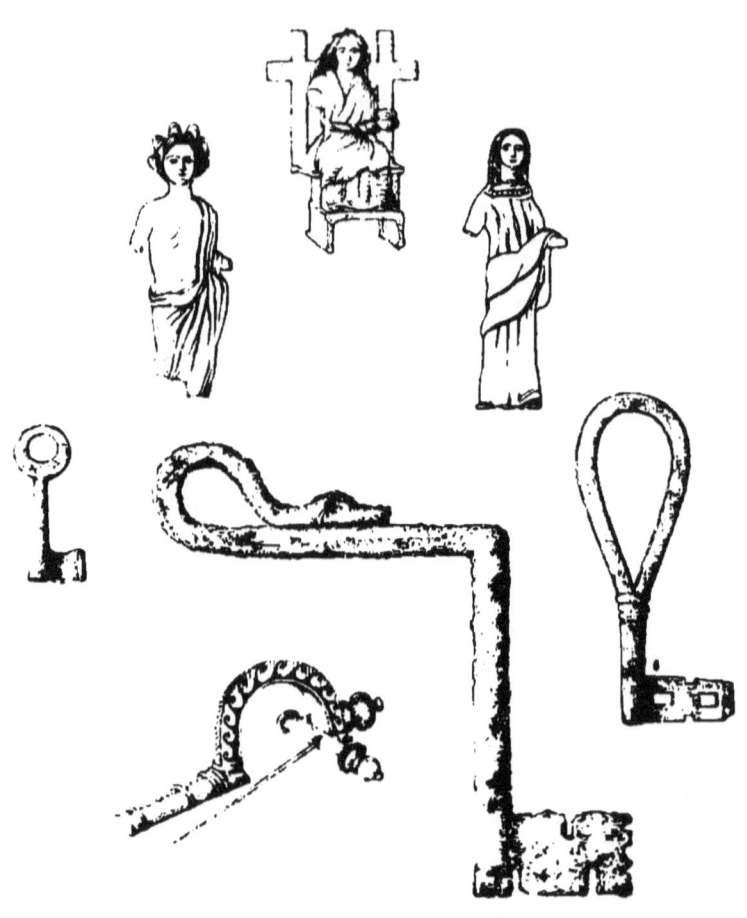

PLATE XXXV.
PENATES, ROMAN KEYS, AND FIBULA.

PENATES.

EVERY Roman family had its peculiar guardian-gods presiding in the interior of the house: the gods and guardians of the *penes*, or domestic and household provisions. Their numbers, names, and race were unknown; but they were invoked under the common designation of PENATES, and their images were placed near the hearth in the Atrium, the interior and partly uncoiled space of the house, where the community life of the family was spent. On the hearth offerings were made to them, the never-extinguished flames of the hearth-fire being always kept burning in their honour, and the family table always spread and furnished for them, with a salt-cellar and some viands. In general the kitchen was dedicated to them. They had the care of the welfare and honour of the family.[1]

Of the Three Penates which are represented in the opposite plate, the seated figure at the head of the page was found on the Borough Walls, A.D. 1824. The two standing figures were found at Weston in 1825. They are of bronze, and are drawn about the actual size.

The largest of the Three Keys given in the centre of the plate was found in Sydney Buildings, Bathwick, at the same time as the Block of Lead, already described. The smallest was found near Freshford, in the neighbourhood of which is the site of a Roman Villa at Ilford. It is not stated in what part of BATH the other Key was found, but it is similar to one figured in Mr. ROACH SMITH's Rom. London.[2]

A Spoon found in Cheap Street is preserved in the Museum of the Literary and Scientific Institution, to which it was presented by the Rev. B. RICHARDSON. Here also are deposited a Fibula found in BATH, two Rings which were discovered in a coffin at Larkhall, and two Bronze Armlets, together with two circular Fibulæ found at Cherry Wells, near Charlcombe. These articles complete the list of household utensils and trinkets discovered in the City; but doubtless very many objects of real interest have fallen into private hands, and are either lost or hoarded up in private collections.

[1] Virg. Æn. i., 707, Serv. Æn. ii., 469. (Gen. and Jew, by Prof. Döllinger.)
[2] See plate xxxviii., fig. ii.

CONSTRUCTION OF HYPOCAUSTS AND TESSELLATED FLOORS.

FEW notices remain of Hypocausts discovered in BATH, and not many of Tessellated Pavements. The most particular and important account of a Hypocaust is that given by Dr. LUCAS at the time of the first discovery of the ancient Roman Baths.[1] The construction of the furnace of this Bath was laid open, and even the burnt fuel was found about the mouth of the furnace. Hypocausts were used, however, not only in public Baths, but for Baths in Roman private houses; and not only for Baths, but for warming apartments, and also for keeping them dry. The suspended floor had not always the accompaniment of flues and hot air, but was used solely for dryness.

The construction of the Hypocaust was simple. It consisted of a floor of concrete placed upon small pillars about 18 inches high. "Roman Floors appear to have been of two classes. Firstly,—Floors elevated above the level of the ground, generally upon a number of small supports or pillars, called *Pilæ*, in which case they received the name of *Suspensuræ*, and were mostly finished with various designs in Tessellæ. Secondly,—Floors formed on the ground, and without supports, also sometimes tessellated, but not always, as these floors belonged to second-class rooms, and were generally in that portion of the house not used for the immediate accommodation of the proprietor."[2] In the suspended floor the ground was first made hard by beating or ramming down gravel, and upon this were placed piles of brick, sometimes of stone; then came a large square brick or tile as a cap to the pilæ; upon these were placed flanged tiles so as to cover the whole floor, and upon these again was laid a bed of concrete, in which the tessellæ were imbedded. Sometimes the pilæ were of rough hewn blocks of stone, and sometimes partly of stone and brick. The concrete was compounded of pounded brick and lime, and was laid about six inches thick and quite even. The flanged tiles upon which the concrete rested, were placed upon the pilæ with the flange downward.

The Roman bricks appear to have been made with the greatest care, and are now, after a lapse of fifteen or sixteen hundred years, as hard as when first taken from the kiln.

[1] See pp., 14, 15.
[2] See Cerinium, pp., 62, 64.

HYPOCAUSTS AND TESSELLATED FLOORS.

Floors without the Hypocaust were generally small in size, but their substratum was prepared with the greatest care, and every means taken to secure dryness. The ground was first rammed down hard for a foundation, upon this was laid a stratum of gravel with broken brick and tile, which was made firm and compact; and then came a layer of concrete, made of pounded brick, lime, and sand, mixed together in a fluid state. "This" says Professor BUCKMAN[1] "accords with the directions given by VITRUVIUS—

Nucleus,
Rudus, } Constituting RUDERATIO.
Statumen.

Upon this Nucleus, Tessellæ were sometimes laid, though frequently dispensed with." Examples of this kind of floor were found when the ground was prepared for building the new portion of the BATH Mineral Water Hospital. The Tessellæ were small cubes varying in size; in coarse pavements that have been laid open in BATH, they are generally about an inch in thickness, but in the finer pavements found in other places they are smaller. Their composition was sometimes natural and sometimes artificial.

The natural cubes were formed of—

Chalk	...	White (colour).
Freestone	...	Cream colour.
„	...	Grey (altered by heat).
Oolite (Wiltshire Pebbles)	...	Yellow.
Old Red Sandstone	...	Chocolate.
Limestone, Lime Lias	...	Slate colour or black.

Artificial—

| Terra Cotta | ... | ... | ... | { Light red.
{ Dark Red.
{ Black. |
| Glass ... ... | ... | | | Transparent Ruby. |

These different colours were worked into a variety of patterns, and sometimes into very beautiful designs, which were laid in the floors of the Roman Villas and public buildings. Cirencester is particularly remarkable for the ornamental character of the pavements found there; and for further description of them I would refer the reader to Prof. BUCKMAN'S and Mr. NEWMARCH's very interesting account of the Tessellated Pavements of Corinium.[2]

[1] See Corinium, p. 69.
[2] See p. 25, and following.

ROMAN TESSELLATED PAVEMENTS FOUND IN BATH.

IT is much to be regretted that no correct record has been kept of the Tessellated Pavements found in BATH. We are indebted to incidental notices for all we know of them. When the Mineral Water Hospital was built, A.D. 1738, some remains of Tessellated Floors were laid bare. WOOD, in his description of BATH,[1] has recorded what he discovered, and given an outline plan of the pattern: he supposed this floor to be the remains of the ancient Prætorium. A Hypocaust was discovered at the same time, and flue tiles of a square form, some six inches in diameter and some nine inches. Near this floor was found a deep pit for ashes, and similar pits were found when the new portion was erected, 1859.

The remains described by WOOD were portions of two floors, covered with Mosaic Pavements, the one six feet broad, the other eighteen feet, and the patterns of the Pavements were formed of circles, like the pavement discovered A.D. 1692, in the grounds of Mr. TOMKINS, at Caerleon.[2] The diameter of the circles in the BATH pavement was two feet nine inches. Two stone steps were found leading into another chamber, two feet six inches rise to each step, and a floor paved with common stone, the level of which was twelve inches higher than the other; also a wall, the thickness of which was two feet three inches. Under the S.W. corner of the Hospital Wheat was found. These Roman Remains were six feet below the present surface of the ground, and betwixt them and the natural soil or gravel was a distance of at least three feet.

[1] Chap. vii., p. 270.
[2] See Camden's Brit.

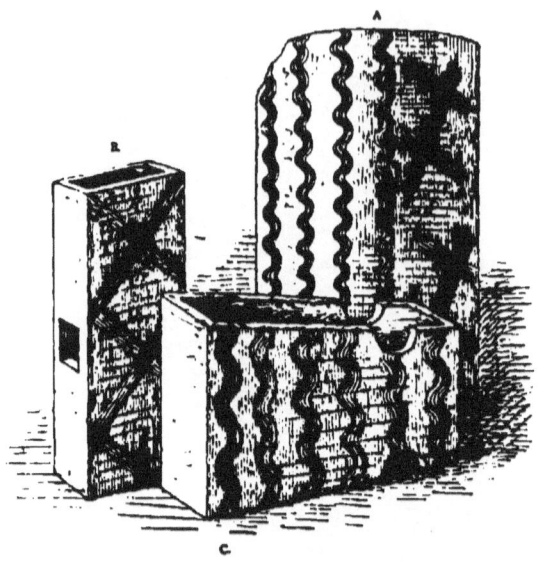

PLATE XXXVI.

    A. ROMAN FLUE TILE, SEMICIRCULAR.
    B. FLUE TILE WITH OPENING ON THE SIDE.
    C. FLUE TILE, WEDGE-SHAPED, WITH CIRCULAR HOLES, AS IF TO ADMIT A PIPE.
    D. PATTERN OF ROM. TESSELLATED PAVEMENT FOUND UNDER THE NEW BUILDING OF THE
        MIN. WATER HOSPITAL.
    E. PATTERN OF PAVEMENT FOUND UNDER BLUE COAT SCHOOL.

When the foundations of the new portion of the Hospital were being dug out, in 1859, another Tessellated floor was discovered. This is now preserved on the site where it was found, in the passage underneath the new building. The pattern is very coarsely executed, and consists of the Labyrinthine Fret, worked out in Tesseræ of white and blue lias. Some other portions of floors constructed of concrete were discernible, and part of the outline of the building to which they had belonged could be traced, by the foundation walls remaining. These floors were sixteen feet under the level of the present City.

Many Roman coins, and a considerable variety of Roman pottery, with bronze and bone implements, and the fragment of an inscription in white marble, already described (p. 75), were found in making these excavations. The coins embraced a period from A.D. 98 to A.D. 408.[1] These Remains were just within the circuit of the ancient Roman walls.

On the site of the present Blue-Coat School, which was rebuilt in 1860, in the same street, another Tessellated Pavement was found. This is now laid down in an anti-chamber of the building, immediately over the spot where it was discovered. The pattern consists of figures of Dolphins and two other animals, one of which is a Sea-horse, and the other has the head and hoofs of a deer, but the hinder part is broken away. One of the dolphins is nearly obliterated. The animals have red streamers flying from different parts of the body, as is common in other pavements found in this country, giving life to the subjects delineated. The Tesseræ are cubes of stone or brick, and the colours red, blue, brown, and white.[2] The pavement, when entire, was probably similar to one found at Cirencester, and described by Prof. BUCKMAN and C. H. NEWMARCH, Esq.[3]

Two Tessellated Floors were laid open in the year 1813. In digging the foundation of a building connected with the premises of Mr. Cruttwell, in the Abbey Green, the workmen came upon a flat surface of masonry, running under the houses on the south side of Swallow Street, at a considerable depth below the level of the present City. On clearing this of the rubbish, it was found to be a Tessellated Pavement, formed of neat cubes about one-third of an inch square, the material being Roman brick and white and blue lias limestone. The pattern of the pavement is said to have been tasteful, but as it ran under an inhabited house, it was impossible to trace the complete design, and the part uncovered was insufficient to give an idea of the whole.[4] It is to be regretted that no drawing has been preserved of the portion uncovered.

[1] See Som. Arch. and N. Hist. Soc. Proceedings. Vol. XI., 1861-2.
[2] See Som. Arch. and N. Hist. Soc. Proceeding, 1861-2, pp. 191 and 192.
[3] Illustrations of the Remains of Roman Art in Cirencester, pp. 30, 33.
[4] See Bath Onwians Gatherum, 20th Aug. 1814.

Another discovery was made in May, 1814, at the S.W. corner of Bridewell Lane, on the premises of Mr. John Allen. Some Imperial Coins were dug up, together with Roman Bricks, and afterwards a Tessellated Pavement was laid bare. Unfortunately, this was hastily broken up before it had been examined by competent persons, but from what remained in fragments, it would appear that it was not of superior elegance in design or workmanship. The materials were similar to those of pavements formerly laid bare.

When the Ancient Roman Baths were discovered, remains of Tessellated Floors were found, but no description of the patterns or figures has been preserved. The examples that remain of Tessellated Pavements discovered within the City Walls are so much inferior in design and execution to those found in other places, and, indeed, to the pavements laid bare on the sites of villas in the neighbourhood of BATH, that they can hardly be accepted as a fair representation of what once existed. The public edifices in AQUÆ SOLIS, if we may judge from the architectural remains, were not inferior to those of other Roman Cities, and the pavements, no doubt, corresponded with the buildings; but those which have been discovered of late years, and the descriptions of those exposed in past times (if we may trust the meagre accounts that remain of them), lead to the inference that they were of late and very inferior workmanship, and do not at all represent the best pavements of AQUÆ SOLIS, since they fall much below the character of those of Roman London or Cirencester. The space within the walls of the city having been so much built upon, has, no doubt, caused the destruction of many patterns, and some may yet remain to reward future inquirers, but those that have been preserved can hardly represent the pavements of the better class of Roman houses. The Rev. THOS. LEMAN, in a MS. note to STUKELEY's Itinerarium Curiosum,¹ says—" Tessellated pavements have been found in every part of Walcot," and it is much to be regretted that no further notice of them has been preserved. Had they been drawn and engraved with the same care as those found at Wellow, we should, no doubt, have had a very interesting collection. The Roman Pavements of Corinium have attracted the notice of all lovers of art, and their design and execution are of a high order of merit.

¹ London, 1721.

PLATE XXXVII.
SMALL ROMAN VASE OF BLACK WARE, FOUND IN THE SYDNEY GARDENS, A.D. 1824.

ROMAN POTTERY FOUND IN BATH.

MANY fragments of Roman Pottery, as might be expected have been found in BATH, but only a few entire Vases. One small Vase, found in the Sydney Gardens, A.D. 1828, is now in the British Museum.[1] The form is that of a cup having a wide and shallow body, which is raised on a stand, and the total height is about 2½ inches, the width 3½, and the depth of the side 1 inch 4 parts. The Pottery is a black glazed ware, resembling Greek, having a red body or paste covered with a black silicious glaze, which is rubbed off at the lower part. The cup appears to be early Roman. The ornament running round the border is the Ivy-leaf, and is rather distorted by the form of the Vase, the contour of which it follows. Small Urns have been found in Stone Coffins, but these are plain in shape, and for the most part formed of dark-coloured earthenware of a coarse kind. The ware most common is the red earthenware, commonly called Samian, some examples of which are given in the accompanying plates.[2] The British Museum possesses specimens of the red ware found in Walcot, and there is also a collection in the Museum of the BATH Literary and Scientific Institution.

Samian ware, in great varieties of pattern, has been found in this Island, and wherever the Roman power extended. It seems to have been employed for domestic purposes, as earthenware and porcelain are now used in this and other countries. The name SAMIAN has been given to it from the Island of Samos having been celebrated for its Potteries for the manufacture of red ware. The Samian Potters were famous about B.C. 900, but it is very doubtful if the red ware found in Britain was manufactured there. It would rather appear to have been made in Italy, Germany, or Gaul. Aretium (modern Arezzo) was famous for its red Pottery, and hence this kind of ware is sometimes called "Aretine Ware."[3]
"At Rheinzabern, situated between Spire and Lauterbourg, towards the French frontier, upon the site of the Tabornæ of the Roman Itineraries, several hundred fragments of the red glazed Pottery, as well as entire vessels, have been exhumed, and with them their moulds, proving that at this locality an extensive manufactory was established. In every respect (observes Mr. ROACH SMITH[4]) most of the engraved specimens are identical with those found in London."

[1] See plate opposite.
[2] See plates xxxviii and xxxix.
[3] See Catalogue of Specimens of British Pottery and Porcelain, by Sir H. de la Beche, C.B. and Trenham Reeks, Museum of Practical Geology; London 1855.
[4] Rom. London, p. 99.

ROMAN POTTERY.

M. SCHWEIGHÆUSER has published a plan of a kiln found near the village of Heiligeuburg, in the valley of the Brucke, about 3 miles from Mutzig, where several kilns have also been disinterred.[1] Near the furnace were found large quantities of fragments of the red Pottery; and upwards of sixteen moulds for vessels, ornamented with bas-reliefs, were discovered.

Mons. BRONGNIART has also recorded discoveries of the remains of kilns at Lezoux, in Auvergne.[2] From Gaul and Germany the ware was imported into Britain.

Roman Potters' kilns have been found in this country, at Normanton Field, Castor, near Peterborough, the ancient Durobrivæ of ANTONINUS,[3] and in the New Forest.[4] The kilns at Castor were discovered A.D. 1822, and vessels and fragments of Pottery were found with them. The ware, however, is different to the red or Samian, and has from its peculiarity obtained the name of DUROBRIVIAN. Vessels composed of this peculiar ware have been discovered at Combe Down, and will be illustrated in subsequent pages of this volume.

The paste of which the red ware is composed, is commonly a compound of silica, mingled with the silicates of alumina and lime; it is usually of a fine vermillion colour, derived from the peroxide of iron, which is supposed to have been purposely introduced into it, and was evidently well worked before being moulded into the shape of the required vessel. The glaze is generally brilliant, unless when decomposed, by being subjected to unfavourable conditions while buried in the earth, and appears to have been formed of a silicate, with an alkalino-earthy base, coloured by peroxide of iron. The ware is commonly well made, and Mons. BRONGNIART observes respecting it, "that it was worked in the most perfect manner, and with the aid of the greater part of the processes and means now employed in the most perfect manufacture."[5] An analysis of different pieces of this ware is given in the Catalogue of the Museum of Practical Geology.[6]

The devices found upon the pottery are very varied, and generally very elegant, including not only fruit, flowers, and leaves, but animals and figures of nearly every kind, musicians playing the lyre, water-carriers, figures bearing baskets on their heads, winged cupids, children at play, gladiators fighting, and men contending with wild beasts. The labours of Hercules form a frequent subject, and a portion of a bowl found in BATH has the

---
[1] Antiquités de Rheinzabern, par J. G. Schweighæuser, Strasbourg, 15 plates 4to.
[2] Traité des Arts Céramiques, Paris, 8vo, 1844
[3] See Durobrivæ of Antoninus, Illustrated, plate xl., fig. 3.
[4] Archæologia, vol xxxv., p. 91.
[5] Essai sur les Arts Céramiques, tom. I., p. 423.
[6] Ceramic Series, pp. 56, 59; 1855.

PLATE XXXVIII.
ROMAN (URN) FOUND IN BATH. (RED WARE.)

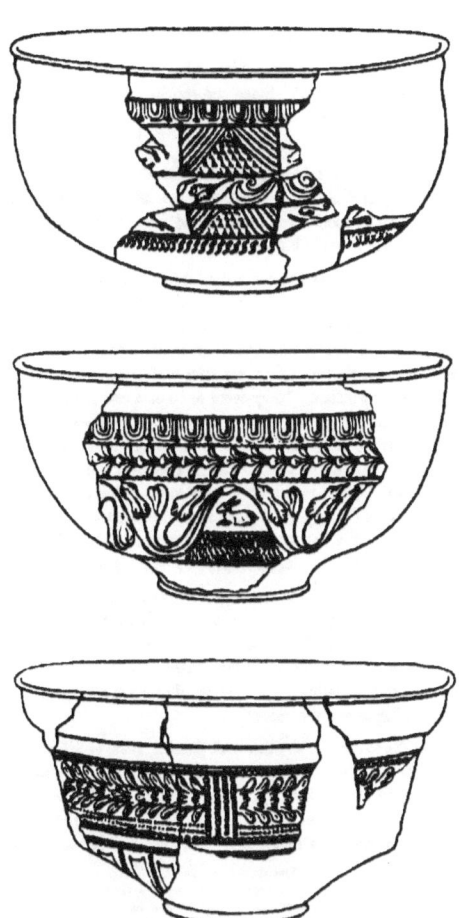

PLATE XXXIX.
SAMIAN BOWLS, RESTORED FROM FRAGMENTS FOUND IN BATH.

figure of Hercules strangling the Nemœan Lion, which he has caught by the head under his right arm, and holds at his mercy.¹ Stags and rabbits are also favourite subjects. The fact of Samian ware being frequently found mended with leaden rivets serves to show the value that was put upon it.

Great interest attaches to this ware on account of its various and beautiful forms. It has been found very plentifully in London, and the British Museum possesses a very large collection of it. Many specimens of vases, and cups and dishes of every description are engraved in Mr. ROACH SMITH's Roman London.²

In some instances, the ornaments, instead of being raised in relief, are incised with great sharpness and skill. Prof. BUCKMAN observes that the shapes of this kind of pottery were exceedingly varied, and most of them very elegant in form, at the same time that we may trace a greater amount of conventionalism than we meet with in the commoner pottery;³ and Mr. BIRCH remarks that all the Vases are wide and open mouthed, and he considers them generally of small proportions. They seem to be of a size generally adapted for table purposes. "Those of the largest dimensions are dishes, paropsides, lances, or paterœ, ornamented with a tendrilled leaf, meant for that of the ivy or vine. They are probably the lances pampinatœ, or hederatœ, dishes with grapes or ivy leaves, such as CLAUDIUS received from GALLIENUS. Some rare dishes, with spouts like mortaria, and bowls with lion headed spouts are known (examples of which are in the British Museum). Occasionally some of the paterœ have handles, the small cups are supposed to be either acetab:!... (vinegar cups), or salinœ, (salt collars). The larger cups are pocula, cyathi, or calices."⁴

Mr. ROACH SMITH states—" In no instances have any vessels of the red glazed Pottery been found in the Kilns discovered in this country or among the unquestionable products of those kilns. Some imitations of the red ware have been found in the neighbourhood of Colchester, but the material is imperfectly tempered and of a whitish hue, with a thin coating of black carbonaceous matter. The vessels of this ware found in England, France, and Germany, are similar in every respect."

Restorations of *Thirteen* Bowls or Vases of Samian ware, of different forms are given in the plates as specimens of the varieties of patterns found in BATH, but the fragments which have been dug up, and the shapes that might be constructed out of them, are very numerous. The following is a list of the Potters' Stamps which have been found upon the red ware. The name of the potter is sometimes followed by an F, for *fecit* (made it) ; or by the letter

¹ See plates xxiv-xxix.
² Illustrations of Roman London, see pp. 90, 91.
³ See Rem. of Rom. Art at Corinium, p. 60.
⁴ Hist. of Ancient Pottery, vol. ii., p. 356.

M, for *manu*, *i.e.*, from his hand, or manufactured by him; and sometimes the letters O or OF *(officina)*, by which it is expressed that it came from the manufactory of such a Potter (as MONTANUS, for example).

POTTERS' STAMPS ON ROMAN RED WARE FOUND IN BATH.

ALBVCI }
CARANTINI. M }.
CASSI........
CORNERTL M.
MINIRIV.
MF. OLIVI
OF. NIG

OVMI....
OF. MODE
PRITANI
SILVI. OF.
SOLE.....
TITVR. OF.

The following is a list of the Pottery found in excavating for the New Part of the Mineral Water Hospital, A.D. 1859—

Cinerary Urn (imperfect).
Bowl of red ware.
Oval Chafing Dish, grey unglazed earthenware.
Fragments of the same.
Small Vase of black Pottery (entire).
Fragments of Samian and other Pottery.
Some Tesseræ.
Six Fragments of Amphoræ.
Seventeen Ditto of light red earthenware (doubtful).
Two perfect Bricks.
One Fragment of Tile, scored.
One ditto Roofing Tile.
Five Fragments of Wall plaster.
One small red coloured Vessel, turned in a lathe.
One elongated Glass Unguentory.[1]

[1] Found on Samian ware, dug up under the New Building of the Mineral Water Hospital.
[2] See Journal of Somerset Archæol. and Nat. Hist. Soc., vol. xi., p. 102.

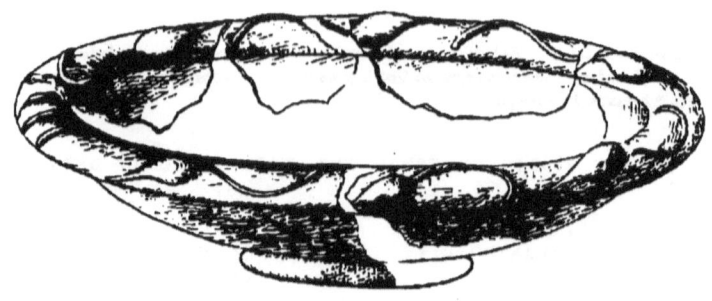

PLATE XL.
ROMAN BOWLS OF SAMIAN WARE, RESTORED FROM FRAGMENTS FOUND IN BATH.

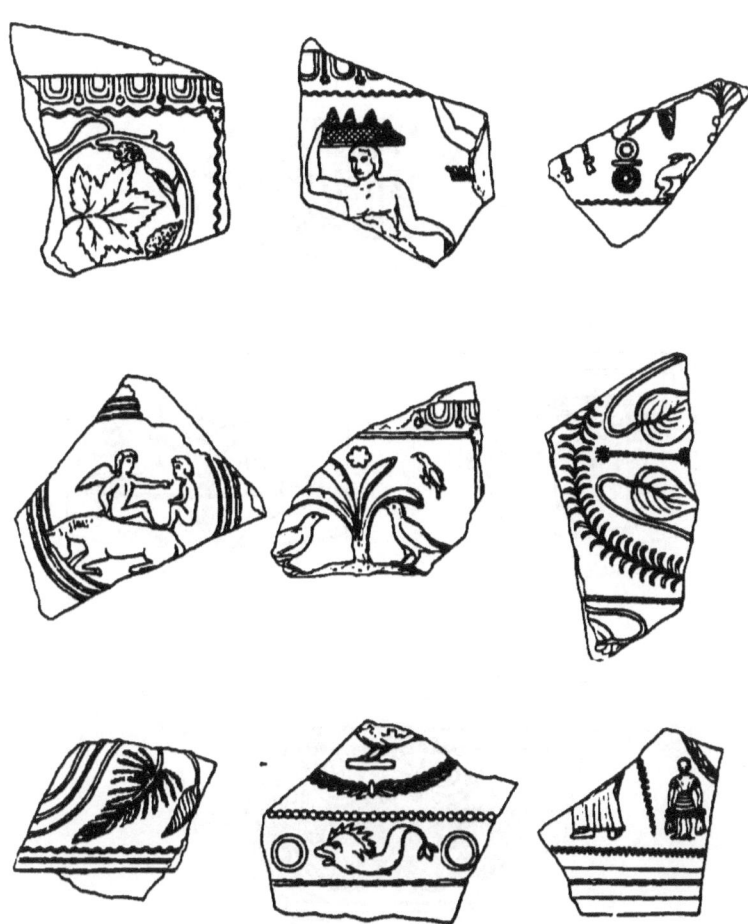

PLATE XLI.
FRAGMENTS OF SAMIAN WARE, FOUND IN BATH.

PLATE XLIII.
SAMIAN WARE, FOUND IN BATH.

PLATE XLII.
SAMIAN WARE, AND PATTERNS ENLARGED.

ROMAN TILES.

MANY large Flue Tiles have been found in BATH and the neighbourhood. These were for the most part discovered on the site of the ancient Roman Baths, and are excellent specimens of their kind. They are preserved in the Museum of the Literary and Scientific Institution. Drawings of some are given as examples.[1] Roman Tiles may be classed as follows :—

    1. Square.
    2. Flanged and notched, made to overlap.
    3. Arched.
    4. Circular pipes, like draining tiles.
    5. Flue Tiles cubic in form, or oblong, with holes in the sides, either square or rounded at the angles.

The Bricks and Flue Tiles are scored on the surface with wavy or curved lines, or with straight lines crossing, the object of which appears to have been to ensure the better adhesion of the mortar. The Flue Tiles were used for the conveyance of heated air through the walls of the apartments, and have openings at the sides, as well as at the ends, where they are connected together.

A semicircular Tile about thirteen inches in diameter, has also been found. Two such Tiles if put together would form part of a Cylindrical Column, and may have been so used, the outside being plastered over with stucco, or they may have formed a wide Cylindrical Flue within the wall. One of these is given in plate No. xxxvi., and also a wedge-shaped Tile, which has two circular holes, one on each side, as if to admit a pipe. This Tile is formed like the key stone of an arch, and measures $9\frac{1}{4}$ inches at the upper portion, and 8 inches at the lower, the height being 13 inches. Flue Tiles have also been found joined together by mortar in pairs, as if forming the curve of an arch. Some of these were discovered in the hypocaust of the Villa at North Wraxall, Wilts.

[1] See plate xxxvi.

ROMAN GLASS.

IT is to be regretted that so little Roman Glass has been preserved in BATH, although much must have been dug up at different times, and probably of fine quality or elegant pattern, if we may judge from two vessels of very elegant form found at Combe Down.[1] Unfortunately no collection has been made, and we are left to conjecture what is lost or dispersed from that found in the neighbourhood of the city. The Ampulla discovered in a Stone Coffin at Swainswick, A.D. 1840, is of very peculiar form.[2] This has been carried out of the City, and is now in the collection of his Grace the DUKE of NORTHUMBERLAND, at Alnwick Castle. A small Unguentory and a few fragments were found when the ground occupied by the new building of the BATH Mineral Water Hospital was cleared for the foundation.[3] These are preserved in the Museum of the Literary and Scientific Institution, which ought to be enriched by every fragment that may in future be discovered either in BATH or in the neighbourhood. Collections of Roman Glass like that contained in the Museum of Practical Geology in Jermyn Street, London, and that at Shrewsbury, from the excavations at Wroxeter, are not only interesting to the antiquary, but useful to the manufacturer.

[1] See plate xlv. A jug or ewer of similar construction is mentioned as having been found at Shefford, Bedfordshire, and a description of it is given in the Archæolog. Journal, vol. i., p. 396.
[2] See plate xlv.
[3] See Journal of Som. Arch. and N. H. Soc., vol. xi., p. 193.

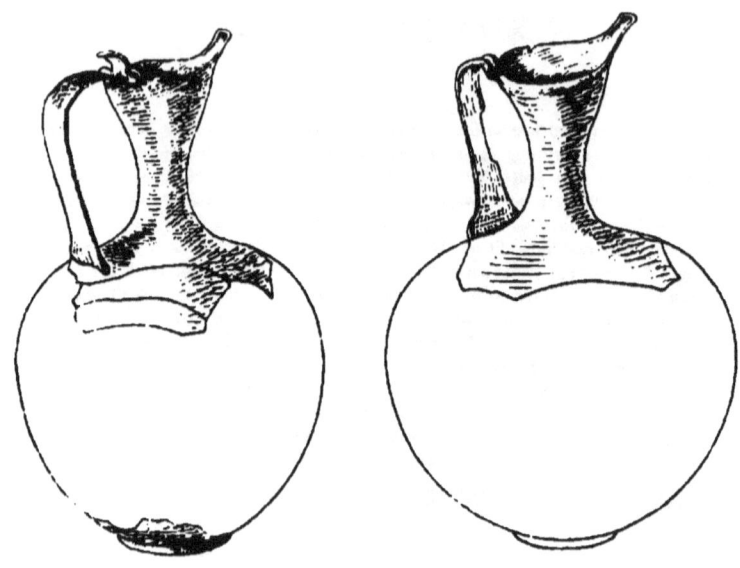

PLATE XLIV.
ROMAN GLASS VESSELS FOUND AT COMBE DOWN, A.D. 1861.   ACTUAL SIZE

PLATE XLV.
ROMAN (AMPULLA) OF GLASS, FOUND IN A STONE COFFIN AT SWAINSWICK,
NEAR BATH, A.D. 1840.   ORIG. SIZE.

ROMAN INTERMENTS.

MANY Interments, apparently Roman, have been discovered in the neighbourhood of BATH; indeed the Coins found with the Remains, and other indications, render it almost a matter of certainty, that with few exceptions, the Stone Coffins and the Earthen Jars found with them, belong to the Roman period, or to the ages that immediately followed the withdrawal of the Roman power.

The writer who first took particular notice of these Funereal Remains, and recorded what he saw, was the learned Dr. MUSGRAVE, who states[1]—" Plurimæ sunt hujusmodi arcæ, nempe lapideæ, apud nos inventæ, nimirum apud Trinobantes, Icenos, et Ordovices ; . . . . non ita pridem ad Aquas Calidas effossa est in suburbiis, juxta Viam qua ad Colliculum itur, *Lansdown* appellatum, ea, quæ Tab. xi. figura prima exprimitur.[2] . . . Fragmentum erat alius Arcæ non procul a Julii Vitalis Sepulcreto erutum, priori non absimile. (A.D. 1706.) . . . . Præter ossa Puellæ[3] quasi decennis omnia, binas tenuit arcella urnulas, singulo latere singulam, et ex luto Imaguncularm ; ut non tantum cadaveri sed et iis, quæ ad illud pertinuerint, accipiendis, inservire has arcellas, arbitramur."

We hence learn that two Interments attracted the notice of Dr. MUSGRAVE ; one on the Road to Lansdown, and the other in Walcot, on the course of the Foss Road, near the spot where the Monument of JULIUS VITALIS was discovered. Dr. MUSGRAVE also remarks that, from the disposition of the bones found in one Interment, the corpse appears to have been placed with the face downwards,[4] and he refers to the wish of DIOGENES the Cynic, to be buried in this position. He also notices that Urns are sometimes found with the opening placed downwards. The Stone Coffins described by Dr. MUSGRAVE appear to have corresponded in size with those which have since been discovered.

[1] Bel. Brit., cap. xviii., § viii.
[2] See drawing in Bel. Brit., cap. xviii.
[3] See Bel. Brit., cap. xviii., § x.
[4] See Bel. Brit., cap. xviii., § ix.

Notices of similar Interments in the neighbourhood of BATH are to be found scattered through various publications of the last century, and a connected narrative of such particulars as could be gathered together, is contained in the Proceedings of the Som. Arch. and N. H. Soc. (1854): from this I shall abridge the following summary, adding some particulars which I have obtained since writing that account, though it is to be feared that many discoveries have been left unrecorded, and that some, which have been placed on record in other publications, may here be omitted.

On the 17th November, 1806, on the south-west side of Trinity Court, near the Turnpike Road, or main Street of Walcot (the ancient Foss Road), some labourers found a hoard of nearly one hundred Roman Coins. 15 were Consular Coins, of different families; 28 VESPASIAN; 13 NERVA; 5 NERO; 15 DOMITIAN; 2 TITUS; 6 TRAJAN. One is stated to have been a Coin of BRUTUS; one of LEPIDVS or AVGVSTVS; and one of JUBA. A few days after, a Medal of NERO, and one of ANTONINVS PIVS were found on the same spot.

March, 1808. In digging the foundation of a new house at St. Catherine's Hermitage, near Lansdown Crescent, Stone Coffins were found. The first was below the walls of an old building, the head being north-east, the Skeleton which it contained was perfect, and 6 feet long; at the feet were iron rivet nails, half-an-inch long, held together by thin plates of metal; some fragments of black Pottery and a few long nails were mixed with the earth inside the Coffin; no Coins were found; outside the cover, on the right hand, lay a Skeleton with the head to the feet of the former; the bones of a large size, and near them the bones of a jaw resembling that of a horse. The head of a second Coffin was to the south-west; on the cover was placed a Skeleton of large size, and with it the handle of a sword and part of the blade, all of iron, much corroded. There was a guard to the handle, like that of a modern cutlass. No Pottery was found with this Interment.[1]

May, 1815. On the premises of Messrs. SAINSBURY and Co., Walcot, two Stone Coffins containing Skeletons were found, one of which was placed with the face downwards, similar to that described by Dr. MUSGRAVE. An Urn, now in the possession of Messrs. SAINSBURY, was also dug up, and two fragments of Samian Pottery. Coins of CLAUDIUS, NERO, VESPASIAN, DOMITIAN, CARAUSIUS, and CONSTANTINE were also discovered; one of the Coins, either that of CLAUDIUS or VESPASIAN, being found inside one of the Coffins. Another Coffin was exhumed in the same year at the back of UPHAM's Library, near the Orange Grove.

A.D. 1815. A Skeleton and a Roman Urn with reticulated lines on it were dug up at the Gas Works.

[1] See a descriptive Paper of Roman Antiq., by Mr. Cranch, read to the Bath Lit. and Phil. Assn., Nov. 11, 1816.

ROMAN INTERMENTS. 99

A.D. 1818. During some excavations made at No. 11, Russell Street, three perfect Skeletons (one of large stature) were found lying beside each other, with several copper Coins of VESPASIAN. At No. 12, a Stone Coffin was found, A.D. 1836 : beneath it were two entire human Skeletons.

A.D. 1822. Two Stone Coffins were found near Burnt House Turnpike Gate (in the line of the Foss Road), and previously to this two others near Claremont Place, Combe Down.

A.D. 1824, June. At Lambridge was found a Sandstone Coffin, of rude construction, containing two Skeletons, one an adult and the other a child ; near the head of the Coffin were two rings of yellow metal (probably bronze), 1½ inches in diameter, narrow and flat, and covered with green patina. Near the Coffin were found three pins, probably used to connect the grave clothes: the larger was 2 inches long, the others were broken.

A.D. 1840. One or two Stone Coffins were found with Skeletons while digging the foundation for St. Stephen's Church.

A.D. 1824, September 21. As workmen were digging out the foundation of an old house in the lane leading to the East Gate, they discovered human bones, and a considerable quantity of Coins, mostly of 3rd brass, of the Emperors GALLIENUS, CLAUDIUS GOTHICUS, TETRICUS, CARAUSIUS, MAXENTIUS, DECENTIUS, and many of CONSTANTINE the Great. The Coins were mostly of the lower Empire, some struck at Treviri, the modern Tréves, and others at Lugdunum, Lyons. Some Roman Pottery and glass was found at the same time.

Previously to A.D. 1819, a Stone Coffin was found in Sydney Buildings, near the Coal Wharf, in the Parish of Bathwick, and afterwards, in that same year, 20 human Skeletons were discovered together, some lying on one side and some on their faces, and in one a large iron nail was found driven quite through the crown of the head. Near one of the Skeletons was a copper box, which opened with a spring, and in it were eight copper coins, all of the lower Empire. Three other Coins, one of the city of Constantinople, and a fine bronze Fibula in a good state of preservation were also discovered. About 40 yards distant was found, at the same time, a Leaden Coffin, containing a perfect male Skeleton, with the head to the east. An ancient road, probably Roman, ran up Bathwick Hill in this direction, and made for Claverton.

The Bath and Cheltenham Gazette (7th October, 1823), contains the following particulars of a further discovery in the same locality :

" At a small depth from the surface, the workmen discovered a stone coffin, rudely finished, lying north and south, the cover of which was composed of various stones, some of which had been removed, and the skull of the person interred taken out and thrown on the outside, near the feet. The remaining bones, much perished, were found in the coffin; among them were several fragments of earthen cups, and a larger one, of fine Samian ware, used probably for libations, had been broken. These, it may be presumed, were placed with the corpse at the time of interment, containing the usual offerings of wine, milk, honey, &c., to the manes or ghost of the deceased, as was customary on such occasions with the Roman and Romano-British inhabitants of this country, before their conversion to Christianity. A Roman coin, small brass, was also found near the coffin, but too much injured by time to be with certainty appropriated to any particular Emperor, but apparently late in the Empire. There was also a glass bead, the size of a common marble, perforated, as if it had formed part of a necklace or bracelet: the rest of the beads no doubt were taken out or lost when the skull was removed, or if any part of them were remaining, they were lost or taken away in the confusion that prevailed at the opening, owing to the great number of persons whom curiosity had drawn to the spot. A small brass hook, apparently a part only of a fibula used to confine some part of the dress, was among the contents of the coffin; from which circumstance, and the beads being a female ornament, added to the smallness of the bones, it may be reasonably inferred that the remains were those of a female deposited there during the time the Romans were in possession of the country."

A few yards from the Coffin a small Silver Coin was picked up, supposed to be British or Gaulish. The Coin was about the size of the Roman denarius, disked: on the obverse a rude head; on the reverse, a horse—a favourite emblem on British Coins. The gentleman into whose hands it fell, presented it to the writer of the account in the Bath and Cheltenham Gazette. A similar Coin is said to have been found near Marshfield, in Gloucestershire, another in Berkshire, and this third in the immediate neighbourhood;—"a strong presumptive proof, it is thought, of their general currency and probable British origin."

A.D. 1861. In making a drain at the foot of Bathwick Hill, at the point of divergence of Sydney Buildings, a pair of Stone Coffins were discovered; one filled with very fine sand, and the other with sand of a coarser kind. The former Coffin contained the Skeleton of a female, and the fine sand on being submitted to microscopic examination revealed minute fragments of coarse woven texture, particles of scoria and bitumen, with small nodules of iron; a small bronze bead, which was perforated, and seemed to have formed part of a necklace, was also found in it. Each Coffin had a cover formed of a single stone, which projected over the sides. The second Coffin, filled with coarse sand, contained the remains of a child apparently about 14 or 15 years of age. A third Coffin was also found which had been disturbed some years earlier, and applied to the purposes of a drain. These Coffins were better hewn, and more symmetrical than those found on other occasions. One was left in its original position, and the other carried to the Literary and Scientific Institution, and placed under the portico. The crania are described by a competent authority as exhibiting the characteristics of the Roman or Romano-British skull. The Coffins were placed nearly east and west, and apparently in the direction of the Roman road, leading out of the East Gate of the city, which once passed up the hill. The fine sand in which the female Skeleton was embedded, does not occur anywhere around BATH, and is supposed to have been brought from the mineral district of the Mendip Hills, as on examination it was found to correspond with that which occurs in some of the ancient mining seams in that district. It was near the same place, in the line of Sydney Buildings, that the Pig of Lead alluded to in page 29, and of which a drawing is given in plate viii., bearing the stamp of the Emperor HADRIAN, was found ; from this it has been conjectured that these Interments may have belonged to persons engaged in working the mines in the Mendip Hills. In sinking a shaft about 20 yards further to the east, some black Pottery of coarse texture, and some red Samian ware was found, together with burnt bones.

In the course of the same year, there was found in the Sydney Gardens,[1] a well-formed Stone Coffin, having the exact shape of one of modern times, being angular at the shoulders and not rounded off at the extreme corners. The lid, which was rounded on the upper surface, exactly fitted the Coffin, and projected over the sides. In it was found a Skeleton, apparently that of a female about 50 years of age. The back teeth of the jaw were worn level at the crown, the furthest were decayed, and two of the front teeth were gone. The bones of the hands seem to have been displaced, and a button or stud much corroded was found under the Coffin lid. The examination of this Interment yielded no further particulars, but it is remarkable that in the Sydney Gardens was found the tomb of the Priest of the goddess Sul, now deposited in the Literary and Scientific Institution, and described page 54. Here also was found the elegant Cup, which is elsewhere engraved. The shape of the Coffin was similar to one found at Caer-Leon, and drawn in Mr. LEE's Book, see plate viii., fig. 7,[2] but the BATH Coffin is of much superior workmanship.

A.D. 1857. An Interment in a Wooden Cist, of which the nails and two fastenings like modern hinges remained, was found in the Villa Fields, on the site of the Gravel pit near the road to Hampton Row. With the bones and skull, three Urns were discovered, two of which were broken, and the Cist had entirely perished, but the Skeleton is said to have been perfect when first discovered.

[1] See Journal of Brit. Arch. Assoc. for 1861, p. 222
[2] Isca Silurum. Illustrated Catalogue.

A.D. 1843. The workmen employed in the construction of the Cemetery in Lyncombe Vale, discovered a Stone Coffin containing human remains, apparently those of a man of deformed stature, from 60 to 70 years of age. The Coffin lay S.S.E., and was found broken, the fracture being occasioned probably by bringing it too quickly in contact with the rock on which it was placed. The lid was also broken, and appeared to have borne some inscription or rudely carved memorial, which could not be deciphered. Afterwards a second Coffin was exhumed, having been found only 14 inches under the turf. The length was 6½ feet, and the Coffin was formed of a single block of oolite, and covered by a heavy lid. The Skeleton, which was more perfect than the former one, was that of a tall man, and the skull exhibited the general characteristics of a Roman cranium. The Coffin was of rude formation, but manifested more care than the other. The sides and massive lid were covered with diagonal lines, but no letters were discovered. Not far from this were found several Roman Coins of brass, one of GALLIENUS, three of CONSTANTINE, one of CARAUSIUS, and two doubtful: a counterfeit Sterling of EDWARD I. is said to have been found at the same time.

May 27th, 1859, another Stone Coffin was found, while making a grave in the same Cemetery, which also contained a Skeleton of large size. The interior of the Coffin was 6 feet 2 inches long, and about 16 inches wide, and the direction of the head S.S.E. The lid consisted of three stones 8 inches thick, and was covered with diagonal lines.

Sept. 10th, 1852, discoveries of Stone Coffins were made in Russell Street, while workmen were employed in making a sewer. They first came upon four, lying in pairs, and nearly parallel, about 2 feet apart, and the lower pair a yard distant from the upper; immediately above them was a Skeleton. In the first Coffin was found a Skeleton of large size, in the next were two skulls and various bones. The smallest Coffin contained no skull, but loose bones. This had no cover; the others had covering stones, one of which was of superior workmanship. In one of the Coffins was found a perfect Skeleton, supposed to be that of a female, lying on the left side, with the right arm crossed over the breast, and the left extended down the side. The Coffin contained also part of the jaw of an infant, a metal pin 10 inches long, much corroded, together with the head of a smaller pin, portions of the jaws of two small animals, and a quantity of bituminous substance. Some fragments of an Earthen Vessel were found at the same time, and a Coin of the Emperor CONSTANTINE, some pieces of Glass, and various Bones of graminivorous animals.

Another Coffin was afterwards found lying in the same direction, and in it a Skeleton of larger size than the others, and on the right side of it near the ribs was placed a small Urn of dark pottery. The Urn is now in the Museum of the Literary and Scientific Institution. Roman Pottery was also discovered.

ROMAN INTERMENTS. 103

This last discovery was followed by a sixth and seventh; the former Stone Coffin contained the Skeletons of two children about 8 or 9 years of age, and near the latter was found the lower stone of a Quern. A Wall taking a north-east direction was also discovered, 3 feet wide at the base. The portion laid bare was about 5 foot in length, and formed part of a semicircle. Some fragments of earthenware were found at the same time, being the bottoms of vessels, marked with the stamp MARTI. and QVINTI. M. In this spot, therefore, eight Stone Coffins have been discovered, besides Skeletons not placed in Coffins, and these Interments, which are always accompanied with the finding of Roman Coins, and placed in pairs, seem to indicate the line of Roman road which entered the city, passing down Russell Street to the North Gate, and which branched off from the Via Julia. The Via Julia continued its course through Weston, and there, also, along the line of its direction, Roman Coins and Interments have been found.

Three or four Stone Coffins are stated to have been found behind Weston Farm House, and a large number were dug up about A.D. 1823, at or near the site of Partis College, which would appear to have been an old burying ground.[1] All these Coffins were of the common trough-shaped form, and made of BATH freestone; they were generally found about one foot under the surface.

In making the new Cemetery at Locksbrook, on the right of the Turnpike road to Bristol, and a little to the south of the line of the Via Julia, two Stone Coffins were dug up in the autumn of 1863, in clearing the surface of a Gravel pit just beyond the lodge of the Cemetery. Skeletons were found in each Coffin, which were of the form common around BATH, being rounded at the head and squared at the foot, with heavy slabs of stone, from six to eight inches thick, for covers. Their position was north and south. In December, in the same year, a Stone Cist, which contained burnt bones, was found near the spot where the Coffins had been uncovered. It was formed of a cubical block of stone, about a foot every way, and hollowed out so as to form a chest, in which the ashes were deposited, and covered with a flat stone. The Cist is similar in shape, but much larger than the one found at Combe Down,[2] which also contained bones reduced to cinders, and is now in the Museum of the Literary and Scientific Institution. No Coin of any kind was found in the Cist, but contiguous to it were remains of coarse black earthenware jars, which appeared to have contained calcined bones. The Skeleton of a horse and several human Skeletons are said to have been found near, all lying on the surface of the gravel. When the discovery of Stone Coffins and Earthen Jars was made at Combe Down, the head of a horse was found enclosed in a Stone Box, rather larger than the Cist found at Locksbrook.

[1] See Proceedings of Som. Archæol., and N. H. Soc., vol. v., 1854.
[2] Idem. p. 61., plate.

In making a grave in the upper part of the new Cemetery in the parish of Bathwick, in January, 1860, a Coin of the Emperor CRISPUS was found lying near a Skeleton, having no doubt been placed there at the time of Interment. This enables us to assign the date of the Interment to that Emperor's reign, A.D. 300—326, or some time subsequent. The body did not appear to have been enclosed in any Coffin, nor oven in a rude Cist, but had been buried in a secluded valley, now called Smallcombe Bottom, in the part that was, until lately, covered with hanging wood, which probably formed part of the original forest that fringed the skirts of the hills around BATH.

Although the Coins and Pottery, as well as form of the Coffins which correspond with those found on the sites of other Roman Cities, seem to point out these Interments as belonging to the Roman period, there is evidence to show that Stone Coffins were used considerably later by the Northern people who succeeded the Romans in the occupation of this country. Thus the following inscription in Rhunic characters, which relates to the burial of a Norse man, is said to be taken from a Church in Sweden, viz., that of Småland Njudingen, East district, parish of Näfoelaië. The reading is as follows :—

Gunnkell satti stein thenna eftir Gunnar füther ainn, son Hrútha : Helgi lagthi hann i stointhró, bróther sinn, á Englandi, i Bathum.

Which is thus translated :—

Gunnkell set this Stone after Gunnar his father, son of Hrutha : Holgi laid him in a Stone Coffin, his brother, in England, in BATH.

A Stone Coffin dug up at Langridge, where remains of a Roman Villa have been found, contained a Skeleton with a Martel do Fer, the weapon being about the date of the Crusades,[1] and the Coffin used for a second interment, which was not uncommon.

The greater number of Stone Coffins, however, occur always with Roman Coins and Roman Pottery. Occasionally a Coin is found in the Coffin, as at Combe Down, where the Jaw of a Skeleton was discoloured by the decomposition of the Coin, which had been placed between the teeth, the Coin itself being too far corroded to admit of decipherment. The Remains found in BATH confirm the observation of Dr. DÖLLINGER that LUCIAN, whose writings for the most part are a pretty faithful mirror of the notions in vogue among his contemporaries, bears testimony to the continuance of the old traditions of the good reaching the Elysian Fields, and the great transgressors finding themselves given up to the Erinnys, in a place of torment, where they were torn by vultures, crushed on the wheel, or otherwise tormented; while such as are neither heavy sinners nor distinguished

[1] See Journal of Brit. Arch. Association, 1897, p. 153.

by their virtues, stray about in the meadows as bodiless shadows, and are fed on the libations and mortuary sacrifices offered at their sepulchres. An obolus for Charon was still placed in the mouth of every dead body.[1]

We have repeated instances of Interments after cremation accompanying interments of the body whole, and we have the bodies usually lying north and south, except where the direction of the road adjoining which the burial took place caused the corpse to be laid east and west. The Interments appear in most instances to have followed the direction of the Roman roads. The position of the body varied, sometimes prone and sometimes supine. The practice of burying in a sitting posture, an instance of which was lately discovered at Charlcombe, A.D. 1863, appear to have been much earlier than the Roman period. Bodies in a similar posture are said to have been found placed in a cleft of the rock in the wood beyond Sham Castle, on Bathwick Hill. The finding of the Skeleton of a horse with the Interments in three instances is singular, and leads to the idea that horses were sacrificed on the occasion of funerals, and that the human bones near those of the horse, may be those of slaves or attendants who were made to share the fate of their master, and supposed to accompany and attend upon him in the World of Spirits.

In examining the sites of Roman Villas around BATH, Interments are always found contiguous to the Villa and within the enclosure that surrounded it.[2] This is strikingly illustrated by the Interments found at Combe Down, and at North Wraxall. The greatest respect seems to have been paid to the remains of the departed. The Romans up to the time of the Laws of the Twelve Tables, kept the Remains of their dead relatives in ashes in their own houses, and veneration for the departed turned them into family gods and guardian spirits, with whose remains or "deposits" the same roof was shared.[3] The same feeling of veneration induced them in after times to find a resting place as near as possible to their former abode.

The constant occurrence of Roman Interments give some idea of the extent of the Roman population, and its diffusion into every quarter around the city. In making new cemeteries, in three instances previous Interments have been found. In two instances, these were accompanied with Roman Coins, and in the third, the mode of interment, and the Remains found, left little doubt of its being Roman or Romano-British. As the process of building goes forward, and as the surface of the land is uncovered, so do we find fresh traces of Roman occupation, and of the firm hold they seem to have had upon the country.

[1] Lorian, de Lart. 7, 8. See Gentile and Jew in the Temple of Christ, by John J. I. Dollinger, Prof Eccl. Hist., Munich, p. 146. Trans. by N. Darnell, M.A. London, 1863
[2] See Somersetshire Arch. and Nat. Hist. Soc. proceedings, 1854, p. 49.
[3] See Dollinger's Jew and Gentile, vol. ii., p. 60.

ROMAN ROADS.

TWO Roman Roads of importance, namely the Foss and that known by the name of the VIA JULIA, passed through AQUÆ SOLIS. The Foss extended from Lincoln to Ilchester, and probably to the Sea Coast at Maridunum (Seaton); the Via Julia passed out of South Wales at the Aust passage and so through BATH to Cunetio, near Marlborough, and to Silchester and London.

"We may reasonably conclude (says Dr. GUEST[1]) that the whole of the Roman Road between Ilchester and Lincoln was known as the Foss during the 12th Century, and probably at a much earlier period, and therefore that in all likelihood the whole of the Road between these termini was protected by the King's Peace during the reign of EDWARD the Confessor." From the Laws of EDWARD the Confessor (revised by him although really made by EDGAR), we learn that there were at that time in England Four great Roads protected by the King's Peace, Watlinge Street, Foss, Rikenilde Street, and Erming Street. The King's Peace was a high privilege; any offence committed on these highways was tried, not in a local court, but before the King's own officers. The privileges of the Four Roads were confirmed by WILLIAM the Conqueror, and continued by his successor, and probably extended to all the highways in the kingdom about the first half of the 12th Century.

"The name Foss," says Dr. GUEST, "has given rise to some very strange hypotheses. It has been supposed that the Road was so called because it was one of the *hollow* ways which marked out the lines of ancient *British* traffic; but the *Roman* character of the Foss is perhaps more decided than that of any other highway in the Island. It has been conjectured by others to have been left *incomplete* by the Romans, the *Fossa* being finished but not the *dorsum* or ridge.

[1] Arch. Journal, June, 1857, vol. xiv., The Four Roman Ways, by Edwin Guest, D.C.L.

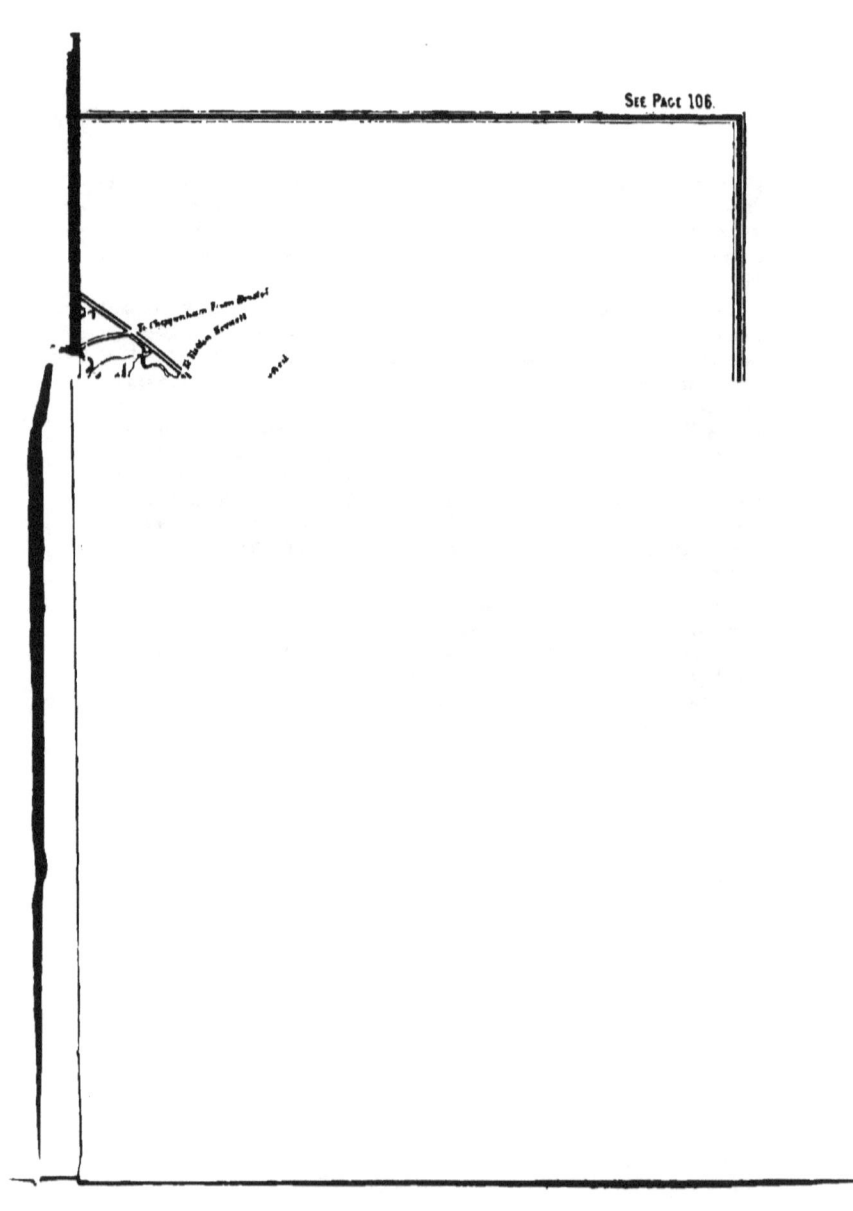

Roman writers upon Agriculture give the name of *fossa* not merely to the open but also to the covered drain. One was called *fossa cœca*, the other *fossa patens*. In constructing a causey the Romans first removed the surface soil, and made a *fossa* to receive the gravel and other hard materials.

>Alto
>Egesta penitus cavare terras
>Mox haustas aliter replere fossas.

It may be that as the *fossa* which served for a covered drain retained the name when filled with stones and brushwood and covered with soil, so the Road-maker's *fossa* kept its name, even when it appeared in a finished causey. The word *fossatum* is used by the later Latinists as a synonym of *fossa*, and employed in charters to denote a causey from the 11th to the 15th Century.

The great Roman Road which we call the Foss, appears to have been termed the *fossa*, κατ' ἐξοχήν—the causey." Such is the explanation given by Dr. GUEST, in his valuable paper on the Four Roman Ways, printed in the Archæological Journal. None of the Roman Itinera describe the *entire* line of the Foss. The 7th and 8th Itinera are carried along a portion of it—from Lindum to Venonæ, but the other portion is not included in any Iter.[1]

From Cirencester to BATH the Foss Road is supposed to coincide nearly with the modern Turnpike Road, which, according to the survey made A D. 1840,[2] is said to present the distinguishing characteristics of a Roman Way, viz., the Road being much raised above the level of the adjoining ground, and for the most part protected by a ditch on each side, of which traces are frequently visible. On the south slope of Banner Down, these distinguishing marks become too vague to be depended upon, but there is a lane still called Foss Lane, which leads straight for AQUÆ SOLIS. Mr. LEMAN in his MS. notes to HORSLEY'S B. R.,[3] has sketched out the entire route, and it is traced by COLLINSON from the point at which it leaves Corinium (Cirencester) to its junction with the Roman Road from Silchester and Marlborough, at Bathcaston. " In approaching BATH," he says, "it runs between Marshfield and Colerne, nearly equi-distant from both, passes the *shire-stones* at the junction of Wilts, Somerset, and Gloucestershire, and crosses Banner Down, descending by the western brow of the hill, where it enters Batheaston. It is called by the country people ' Long Lane,' and may be traversed.[4]

[1] See Som. Arch. and N. H. S. proceedings, vol. xi., p. 177.
[2] See United Service Journal for 1840, p. 566.
[3] See copy of B. R., Bath Lit. and S. I.
[4] See Collinson's Hist. of Somerset, vol. i.

From its union at Batheaston with the Roman Road from Silchester, it passed along Walcot, where Roman Interments and portions of Funereal Stones have been found. The line of Roman Road is then supposed to have passed up Guinea Lane, and continued to the head of Russell Street. At this point the two Roads which had united diverged, and the Foss Road passed through the North Gate into the City, and left it again by the South Gate, and then crossing the River by a bridge, continued its course up Holloway, till it fell in with the present Wells Road a short distance before reaching the Turnpike Gate. From thence it continued past Bloomfield Place and Cottage Crescent, over Odd Down, crossing Wansdyke at the next Turnpike Gate, where it again coincides for a short distance with the Wells Road, but leaves it again before arriving at Dunkerton. At the Inn just before the brook is crossed by a bridge, the roads coincide, and continue nearly in company to the Red Post Inn, near Camerton Park, a mile beyond which point Roman Remains have been found. The course is well laid down in the Ordnance Map. Remains of Roman Villas mark the line of this ancient Road, as will be seen in the chapter on Villas.

The other Roman Road, which is known as the Via Julia, and passed out of South Wales, coming from Caer Leon and Caerwent to the Severn, crossed it at a point which has been the subject of much discussion. The difficulties are clearly stated by Mr. ORMEROD.[1] *Aust*, however, seems to have the best claim to be considered the usual ferry in the Roman age.[2]

The 14th Iter is carried along the Via Julia, " Ab Isca Calleva," and we have the different Stations mentioned, of which AQUÆ SOLIS is one. Thus —

Item alio itinere, Ab Isca Calleva, M. P. ciii. sic.

Venta Silurum	...	Caerwent	M. P. viiii.
2. Abone	...	Bitton	M. P. viiii.
1. Trajectus	...	Sea Mills	M. P. viiii.
AQUIS SOLIS	...	BATH	M. P. vi.
Verlucione	...	High Field, near Sandy Lane	M. P. xv.
Cunetione	...	Folly Farm, near Marlborough	M. P. xx.
Spinis	...	Spene	M. P. xv.
Callova	...	Silchester	M. P. xv.

The modern names are taken from LEMAN'S MS. Notes to HORSLEY'S Brit. Rom., and it is proposed to transpose the names of *Abone* and *Trajectus*. HORSLEY observes "it is generally supposed that there has been a transposition of the names Trajectus and Abone,

[1] See Omerod's Strigulensis, p. 20 et seq.
[2] See Strigulensis, p. 21.

but I see no necessity (says he) for this alteration. Trajectus may perhaps relate to the passage over the Avon." Whoever has examined the Station at ABONE can hardly consider that the passage of the Avon at that point, which would be accomplished by an ordinary bridge, could acquire the name of TRAJECTUS, unless the conditions of the country have greatly altered, and the River in ancient times was much wider than at present. If the authority of RICHARD in his Itinerary may be at all relied upon, there is no doubt that a transposition of names has taken place. The 11th Iter of RICHARD of Cirencester contains the *Via Julia*.

RICHARD, who was a native of Cirencester, and a Monk of Westminster, professed to have collected his materials from Roman fragments, PTOLEMY, and other sources. The History of the discovery of the MS. by BERTRAM is contained in his Tres Scriptores, STUKELEY's Memoir, REYNOLD's Antonine, and BRITTON's Life of HATCHER.

Iter xi.[1] proceeds thus from BATH:—

  Ad Abonam ... ... M. P. vi.
  Ad Sabrinam ... ... M. P. vi.
    unde Trajectu intras in Britanniam Secundam et
  Stationem Trajectam ... ... M. P. iii.
  Venta Silurum ... ... M. P. viii.
  Isca Colonia ... ... M. P. ix.

It will be seen that this differs from the Iter of ANTONINUS, the stations of Abone and Trajectus being here transposed, ABONE coming before TRAJECTUS, and being the first Station after AQUÆ SOLIS, whereas in ANTONINUS it is the second. This correction is proposed by Mr. LEMAN to make the two Iters agree.

"In the first stage, vi. miles," says Mr. ORMEROD, "would agree with placing AD ABONAM at Bitton. The next vi. miles, to AD SABRINAM, would neither reach the Severn nor any known Station near it. Three miles from Aust (if this place is intended) would agree with a passage from thence to the landing place at Blackrock, near to Sudbrook Camp," considered by SAYER[2] to be RICHARD's " Statio Trajectus," which agrees with RICHARD as to being on the western shore, or in Britannia Secunda. If, therefore, GALE's transposition of TRAJECTUS and ABONE be adopted, placing *Abone* " ad ripam Abonis fluvii," and we limit the meaning of *Trajectus* to an estuary or river broad enough to require the aid of navigation, we may obtain something like a solution of the difficulty, but, as Mr. ORMEROD observes,

[1] Bertram, p. 39.
[2] Hist. of Bristol.

"Where numerals are corrupted, and the very ruins and vestiges of former Roads have disappeared, precise confirmation is hopeless." The Via Julia, therefore, may be traced thus—Coming from Calleva (Silchester) it passed through Cunetio, (Folly Farm, near Marlborough), and coinciding with the ancient line of the Wansdike at *Morgan's* Hill,[1] passed on to Farley Down, and afterwards entered the valley of the Avon just below Bathford to the south of the Church. Before entering the village of Batheaston it met the Foss way, and united together they continued on through the suburb of Walcot, till they parted company at the head of Russell Street, from whence the Via Julia continued on through Weston, and passing by Northstoke pointed direct for Bitton, where it entered the Roman Station, a portion of which still exists. For the remainder of its route from thence I must refer to Mr. ORMEROD's Memoir, to COX's Monmouthshire, i., p. 14, and to SAYER's Bristol, i., p. 151.

It seems most probable that a Roman Road led from the West Gate of the City, across the Victoria Park, and joined the Via Julia before reaching Weston. Roman Remains have been found in the Park, which seem to point to a road in that direction. During excavations in the Park for gravel, a fine large Roman Fibula was found, pierced and plated with gold, said to be now in the possession of the EARL of CADOGAN; also a small Sword Belt, with a buckle attached to the lower vertebræ of the back of a Skeleton found there. At the same time a large Tusk of Ivory was discovered. In digging the new road at the entrance of the Park from Queen Square, *Eight Sepulchral Urns* were found, together with lacrymatories, several pieces of Armour, Beads, and portions of a Cæstus. This is strong confirmatory proof of a Road having passed this way, since burials are always found on the sides of the public Roads, outside the Roman cities.

Another Road, the traces of which can only be discerned by the Interments which have been found, seems to have passed up Bathwick Hill, after crossing the River near where the present Mills are situated. At the foot of Bathwick Hill many interments, as well as Roman Coins and Pottery have been found ; also in the Sydney Gardens ; and it is probable that the direction of the Roman Road was marked by an old Road which formerly passed up the Hill, crossing the site of Sydney Buildings, and reaching the top of the Hill not far from the point where the four Roads at present meet. In the Fields to the north of the present Road to Claverton, were formerly traces of an old Road, which pointed direct to the Ferry at Warleigh. The Road from that Ferry to the Dry Arch, which is now a deep Lane, is known among the peasants as the old Roman Road, and can be traced to Monkton Farley, beyond which it fell into the Roman Road to Marlborough and Silchester.

[1] See Som. Arch and N. Hist. Soc proceedings, vol. vii., 1856; Sir R. C. Hoare's Anc. Wilts, vol. ii.; Stukeley's Itin, Cur., p. 113

It is to be regretted that no notes have been taken of the traces of VICINAL Roads in the neighbourhood of BATH. These have occasionally been met with ; and as I am informed, distinct traces have been found on Lansdown. Could these have been noted down, and their direction marked in a map, we might have succeeded in recovering the traces of many which are now entirely lost. The great lines of Roman Road are clearly ascertained, but the Vicinal Roads, of which there were doubtless many, have all disappeared, and, it is to be feared, beyond recovery.

VESTIGES OF ROMAN VILLAS

WHICH HAVE BEEN
DISCOVERED IN THE VICINITY OF AQUÆ SOLIS.

THE Roman Remains found in BATH entitle it to the rank of one the most elegant Roman Cities in Britain, but the Villas, traces of which have been found in the immediate neighbourhood, give a still greater idea of its opulence and security. These Villas, although mentioned incidentally by different writers, have never been collected into one record: two or three have been fully described, but the notices of the rest are very meagre. It is intended in this volume to give some idea of the number that existed within a radius of seven miles of the city, or a little beyond, to bring together the fragmentary notices which are found in various publications, and to record the latest discoveries.

Villas are for the most part found situated either on the line of the Foss, as it approached BATH from Cirencester, or quitted it for Ilchester; or on the Via Julia, which coming from Marlborough, passed through BATH, and then led to the Trajectus, or passage across the Severn.

The largest and most interesting Villa is that discovered at Wellow, four miles south of BATH, and on the line of the Foss Road to Ilchester.[1] The ground plan has been carefully laid down, and the pavements drawn by the late Rev. JOHN SKINNER, Rector of Camerton, and published 1st January, 1823, the engravings being executed by H. and E. WEDDELL.

[1] Collinson (Hist. of Som., p. 325) says, of Wellow—"This place, lying so contiguous to the Foss, and so near to Aquæ Solis of the Romans, was one of the most considerable Villas. There is a spot called Wellow Hayes, where no less than four Tessellated Pavements were found. The first A.D. 1685 (see Gale's Antoninus, p. 69.; the others, A.D. 1737 and 1739. At the same time were discovered remains of a Roman Sudatory, in which were fragments of potery and other utensils."

The plan of this Villa formed three sides of a quadrangular court, 150 ft. by 190, the shorter side facing the south, and at the further end of this court were the principal rooms. Here were found the Tessellated floors, the largest being 34 feet by 26, but the upper part of the border only is now remaining. This pavement had been repaired at a subsequent period, in a manner not corresponding with the original design, and betokening a want of knowledge of the art of Mosaic. On each side of this central chamber were Passages 26 ft. by 6 ft., the floors being laid in Mosaic. These are given in Mr. Skinner's plates. Two Chambers on each side adjoined these passages, and beyond these were Passages with Hypocausts, for the purpose of warming the apartments. In front, and at the back of the chambers were long Galleries or Crypto-portici, the upper one measuring 156 ft. by 12 ft. in width, and the lower probably the same length by 10 feet in width. The pavement was formed of white lias and pennant stone.

These Crypto-portici were places of exercise, and are the origin of the mediæval cloister. At the end of the upper one is a Chamber, 20 ft. by 15 ft., having an elegant Pavement, the design of which is also given in Mr. Skinner's plates.[1] In it are four animals, two at each end of the central space, the centre itself being a very elegant fret. At the side of this apartment a Hypocaust was discovered, and another at the further end of the upper Crypto-porticus.

To the west of these apartments was the wing containing the Baths, the Chambers pertaining to them, and other offices. On the opposite side of the court appear to have been Stoves for smelting iron and lead ore, pieces of these metals having been found close to the flues, some fused, some not. Adjoining the apartments were others, probably for the artificers, as quantities of coarse Pottery were found intermixed with the scoria near the stoves.

A Wall extended to the north of the Villa at Wellow, and probably enclosed a certain space of ground, which might serve as an orchard, a garden, or a small paddock. This is also the case at North Wraxall, near Castle Combe, where the Wall was traced throughout. Within this enclosure, about 250 or 300 feet above the level of the Villa, was the spring that supplied it with water. Near the boundary Wall, quantities of bones of animals, pigs, sheep, deer, oxen, &c., were found; also oyster shells, cockles, and other shell fish.

Roofing Tiles, ridge Tiles, and a freestone Pinnacle, 13 in. in height, figured in Mr. Skinner's plate, were found. A similar Pinnacle was discovered at North Wraxall, and Collinson states that large Stones were found, some round and others square, being

[1] See plate No. iv.

part of the edifice. The British Museum possesses a fragment in bas-relief, found on the site of this Villa, which was presented to the Museum by the Archæological Institute in 1851. The subject is composed of three figures,[1] two female and one male. The female figures are draped, and the one holds in her left hand a staff or forked instrument. The male figure appears unclad, except that the chlamys is thrown over his left shoulder, and he holds an apple or other fruit in his hand.[2] COLLINSON states that previously to the publication of his History in 1791, several Stone Coffins were found in a barrow near the Villa.[3]

VILLA NEAR NEWTON ST. LOE.—The next Villa which deserves attention was discovered in making the line of the Great Western Railway between BATH and Bristol, and is situated near the Avon just below Kelston Park.

Happily a careful account was drawn up at the time from personal observation, and published by the Rev. W. L. NICHOLS, M.A., in 1838, under the title of "Horæ Romanæ." In the Introduction he states that remains were found of "two distinct buildings situated on a gentle slope overlooking the beautiful reach of the River Avon, which lies immediately under Kelston Park." The walls of both were formed of the rough lias of the neighbourhood. The lower structure alone presented any feature of interest, and is described as consisting of a range of buildings measuring 102 ft. by 55 ft., but the original length was greater, "one extremity having been cut through by the Bristol Road, which bounded the ruins to the North." The entrance was on the East side, and opened upon a long corridor, like that described as existing in the previous Villa, which reached the whole length of the building, and led to the various apartments. It was beautifully paved in Mosaic work. A correct plan, with the drawings of the pavements, was made of the portions of the Villa remaining, which have also been published,[4] but in a style much inferior to those by Mr. SKINNER, and it is to be regretted that a larger plan, with more finished drawings, had not accompanied Mr. NICHOLS' valuable notice. Close to the wall of the Turnpike Road were the remains of a Hypocaust, and adjoining it an apartment, probably the Sudatorium, in the centre of which was a large square pillar of stone; the brick flues might still be traced. The principal apartment, the Triclinium, measured only 17 ft. by 15 ft., but seems to have been united to an adjoining room of nearly equal dimensions, though perhaps capable of being separated by folding doors, or an aulæum or curtain. The floor of the Triclinium was ornamented with a Tessellated Pavement, in perfect preservation. This was removed and placed in the Railway Station, at Keynsham, but afterwards taken to Bristol. An

[1] See plate xlvi.
[2] See Archæol. Journal, v. iv. p. 356.
[3] See also Phelps's Hist. of Somerset, vol. ii. p. 164.
[4] See Description of the Roman Villa, with its Tessellated Pavements, discovered at Newton St. Loe, Twerton, near Bath. Bath: W. Cook, 7, Grove Street. London: Monroe, 31, Strand, 1839.

PLATE XLVI.
FRAGMENT OF SCULPTURE FOUND AT WELLOW

PLATE XLVII.
TESSELLATED PAVEMENT FOUND AT NEWTON ST LOE.

application was made by the BATH Literary and Scientific Institution to obtain it for the vestibule of that building, but without effect. A faithful drawing of it, however, was presented to the Literary and Scientific Institution by the Rev. Mr. NICHOLS.[1] In the centre of this pavement is a circular compartment, bordered by the Guilloche, and within the circle a male figure playing with the hand on a Lyre-shaped instrument. A dog, or some other animal is fawning on him, and in a surrounding compartment formed by a concentric circle of larger dimensions, are represented the stag, the bull, the goat, the leopard, the panther, and the lion, a tree being placed in the upper portion between each figure. Architectural frets of various kinds complete the plan. The central figure may be either Orpheus or Apollo.

The principal Triclinium of the Roman houses was sometimes called " the Apollo." The adjoining room had pavements of a simpler kind, but these having been indented by the fall of the roof, were not in so fine a state of preservation. The Tessellæ used in the work are of five different colours, all from materials found in the vicinity.[2]

Fragments of Pottery, pieces of Fresco painting on plaster, and Glass, similar to our window glass, were dug up; as also Roman Coins, one of silver, of the Emperor MACRINUS, and one of gold, of HONORIUS, A.D. 395. As HONORIUS died A.D. 423, the Villa, (as Mr. NICHOLS observes), must have been inhabited as late as his reign, and probably till the Romans withdrew from Britain, about A.D. 426. Brass Coins of CONSTANS and VALENTINIAN were found.

It is to be regretted that the entire plan of this interesting Villa could not be recovered, and that no notice has been preserved of the portion laid open when the Bristol Road was made. Part of it may still lie buried, to reward the labours of succeeding Antiquaries. A Poem accompanies Mr. NICHOLS's Memoir, with classical notes, which add much to the value of his publication.

VILLA AT COMBE DOWN.—The next Villa demanding our notice is at Combe Down, where recent preparations for building, and quarrying stone, have laid open the site of a Villa, which is not mentioned either by COLLINSON or PHELPS, though SKINNER supposes a fort of Roman construction to have stood there.

The owner of the property, Mr. CRUICKSHANK, has carefully preserved every relic, and collected a small, though very interesting Museum, an account of some of the contents of which has lately been published in the Journal of the British Archæological Association.[3]

[1] See plate xlvii.
[2] See Horæ Romanæ, p. 5.
[3] See Journal of British Archæol. Association, 31st March, 1863.

Here was found the Inscription given page 75,[1] published in the proceedings of the Somersetshire Archæological and Natural History Society.[2] Some Stone Coffins had been discovered here in 1822, and the Rev. RICHARD WARNER supposed the traces of walls which he found to be those of a Roman Station;[3] but subsequent examination of the spot leads to the belief that it was a Villa, although the Inscription found commemorates the restoration of the officers' quarters.

Whether this choice spot may have been a Sanatorium for convalescent Roman officers or not, is a point open to conjecture; at the present day Combe Down is remarkable for the salubrity of the air. There are no remains of a fortified Camp here, though Mr. SKINNER speaks of one,[4] but simply indications of a Villa.

The recent discovery[5] took place, A.D. 1854, in making the garden of the Villa now occupied by Mr. CRUICKSHANK; there three Stone Coffins were found, with broken Pottery, a perfect small Earthen Vessel, and a Coin of LICINIUS. The Coffins were placed north and south, the feet being to the south. This indicated that the interments were heathen. With these Coffins were also found a Stone Chest containing the head of a horse; and another, much smaller, containing burnt bones, now in the Museum of the BATH Literary and Scientific Institution. A similar interment of a horse's head in a Stone Cist was discovered some years since in a Tumulus on the line of Roman road, passing under Wooton-under-Edge, from Cirencester to the passage over the Severn.

A short time afterwards a further Interment was discovered about 47 feet north of the previous one, consisting of a pair of Stone Coffins lying side by side containing Skeletons, in the jaw of one of which was a small brass Coin, which had discoloured the jaw-bone. The Coin could not be deciphered, but was apparently Roman. The Stone containing the Inscription before referred to had been used as a Covering Stone to one of the Coffins, and the Inscription having been placed with the surface downwards had escaped obliteration, although decay rendered it difficult to decipher. Since this discovery the ground immediately below has been taken for a quarry and the surface destroyed, but the clearing of the ground at different times has laid open the whole ground plan of the Villa. No proper plan having been made as the portions were laid bare, I am obliged to describe what remained from notes taken at the time.

[1] See plate xxix.
[2] Vol. v., 1854, and Appendix.
[3] See Letter to the Bath and Cheltenham Gazette, April 22, 1822.
[4] See Phelps' Hist. of Somerset, vol. L.
[5] See Som. Arch. Journal, vol. v., pp. 59, 60.

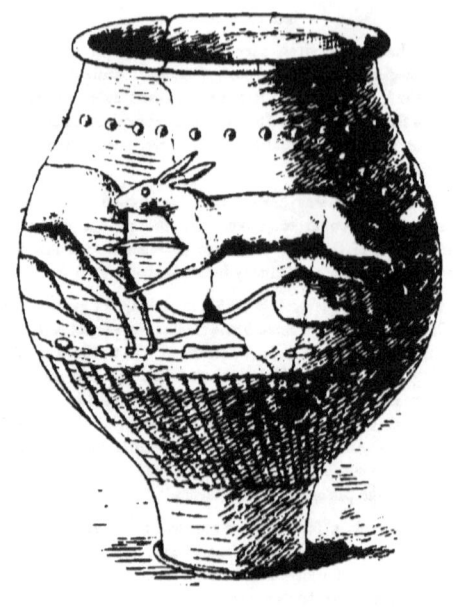

PLATE XLVIII.
ROMAN CUP FOUND AT COMBE DOWN.—ACTUAL SIZE.

PLATE XLIX.
ROMAN CUP FOUND AT COMBE DOWN.—ACTUAL SIZE.

ROMAN VILLAS.   117

1. An oblong portion consisting of three rooms running north and south. Here no floors were found, but simply the outer walls could be traced. Roofing Tiles were found in abundance, and a few copper Coins, together with bones and burnt matter.

2. At right angles to those rooms there seems to have been another set, as the remains of walls were found, and traces of a Hypocaust. These floors were opened in December, January, and February, 1860. On the side of the hill the rock had been cut away to the depth of eight feet, and grooves remained in it as if to admit woodwork; also portions of the rock were left at intervals as piles to support the concrete floor, pieces of which remained here and there; other parts of the floor were supported on tiles piled up in the usual manner, which were set about three feet apart. The size of this apartment was 30 ft. east and west by 18 ft. north and south, and adjoining it another 30 ft. by 10 ft.; small pieces of stucco were found adhering to the walls. These rooms were 20 paces distant from the portion first opened, and give the idea that this Villa had been built round an open court and formed three sides of a square. The remains of an entrance gate on the east side of the Villa were traced. During the excavations 230 Roman Coins, chiefly small brass, and nearly all of the later Empire, were found. These are now in the possession of Mr. CRUICKSHANK.[1]

But the most interesting discovery made in opening this Villa was that of the Glass and remains of Fictilia which were found during the spring of 1863, lying just outside the building embedded in mould formed by the decomposition of burnt matter, and which have been engraved and published by the Archæological Association in their Journal for March, 1863. At the request of the Committee the remains were sent to London, and laid before the Association.

These are classed as follows by their Hon. Sec., Mr. SYER CUMING :—

Animal Remains.—Horns of oxen of large size. Large oyster shell.

Lithic Remains.—Pumice Stone, very abundant. Spherical ball, two inches diameter, Cos or hone. *Pistillum* or pestle.[2]

Fictilia.—Pottery of every kind. Fragments of *amphora*. Part of a *colum* or strainer. Two fine drinking cups of *Durobrivian* ware coated with black oxide of iron, embossed with hares, boars, and deer, mingled with tendrils of ivy, a plant sacred to Bacchus.[3] One of these *pocula* is four inches and five-eighths in height, the other six inches in height. They were both found at the bottom of a square building measuring about seven feet by three. Of *Samian* ware there are pieces both plain and embossed, some bearing the makers' names, CINI.M.F. and SACRINI.M. Another object in terra cotta is the *verticillus*, or turbo of a *fusus*, a sure indication that the art of spinning was not neglected by the female members of the ancient domus.[4]

[1] See list contained in chapter on Roman Coins found in Bath and the neighbourhood.
[2] For a notice of ancient pestles, see Journal of British Archæo. Association, vol. vii., p. 63.
[3] See plates xlvii. and xlix.
[4] For a notice of ancient spindles, see Journal of Brit Archæol. Association, vol. xv., p. 365.

Vitrea.—Portions of several vessels of delicate colourless glass, among them remains of *gutturnii*, with loop handles and attenuated lips of most peculiar form.[1]

Bronze.—Vessels of this metal are rarely met with in England, but with the pecula already mentioned was found the mouth of an *ampulla*, one inch and five-eighths in diameter. Other articles of table furniture are presented in *cochlearia*, the bowls of which are, as usual, set below the line of the handle. One[2] has been plated with silver, and has an oval bowl and sharp pointed handle; the first for eating eggs, the second for extracting fish from the shell, as we are told in one of MARTIAL'S *Epigrammata*.

" Sum cochleis habilis, sed nec minus utilis ovis:
Namquid scis potius cur cochleare vocer ?"

A *tintinnabulum*, of hemispherical form, appears to be one of those which were suspended to the breast-belt of the horse.[3] The sheep's bell was of taller make, and frequently four-sided, and the bells for household use were of larger size and meaner fabric. Of *stili*, employed to write upon the waxen *pugillares*, there are two delicate examples, the blade of one being ovate, the other like the ploughman's *vallum*, and graven with a few transverse lines.[4] The blade was for the purpose of erasing the legend when a correction was needed, or the whole surface of the *tabulae* was required for fresh writings. The *stilus* was frequently called *graphium*, of which also mention is made by MARTIAL.[5]

" Haec tibi erunt armata suo graphiaria ferro:
Si puero donas, non leve munus erit."

A pair of *valvellae*, nearly one and three-quarters of an inch in length, resembles examples frequently found on the sites of Roman occupation.[6] Among several *armillae* there is one composed of two intertwined wires, bringing to mind the funicular torches of the Celts;[7] and what appears to be a fragment of another formed of bone, less than a quarter of an inch wide, bound round with a strip of bronze. There are also studs or bosses, one (one inch and six-tenths in diameter) exhibiting traces of green enamel in the sunken portion of the field, which has a shank at the back for attachment to the habit or belt.[8] Of *fibulae* there are no less than ten examples, all more or less harp-shaped, but differing in details.[9] The larger has a hoop at the top to which was once affixed a chain or chord to secure it to the dress of the wearer, and thus prevent its being lost.[10] The smaller specimen still retains much of the silver with which its front was originally plated.

Iron Remains.—These, though few in number, are very curious. Among them are two keys, one of which[11] is here given. A pendant from horse furniture is also a very singular article. It is a triangular plate with loop at top, and four ornamental drops hanging from the lower edge.[12] There are four iron rings which when perfect must have measured nearly two inches in width, and three inches in diameter. What purpose they fulfilled is very uncertain, but they may probably have surrounded a shaft, like the mast of a small vessel. The last, but not the least, interesting iron relic from this locality, is the head of a Teutonic *herv-strel*, or war-dart,[13] five and a quarter inches in length, the socket being open up the side, as in the examples of Anglo-Saxon weapons described in the Journal of Brit. Archaeol. Association.[14] All the iron remains are unquestionably of late date, and seem to indicate that the spot had been occupied by the Teutons after its abandonment by the Romano-British family.

[1] See plate xliv. [2] See plate No. 1., fig. 4.
[3] See fig. 2. [4] See figs. 3 and 4.
[5] Epig., xiv., 21.
[6] See Journal Brit. Archaeol Association., vol. xvii., p. 226.
[7] See fig. 5. Journal Brit. Archaeol Association, vol. xv., p. 236.
[8] See fig. 6.
[9] These presenting most novelty are shown in figs. 7 and 8.
[10] For a notice of fibulae with similar loops, see Journal Brit. Archaeol. Association, vol. xvi., p. 271; xviii., 379.
[11] See fig. 9. [12] See fig. 10.
[13] See fig. 11. [14] Vol. xiii., p. 203.

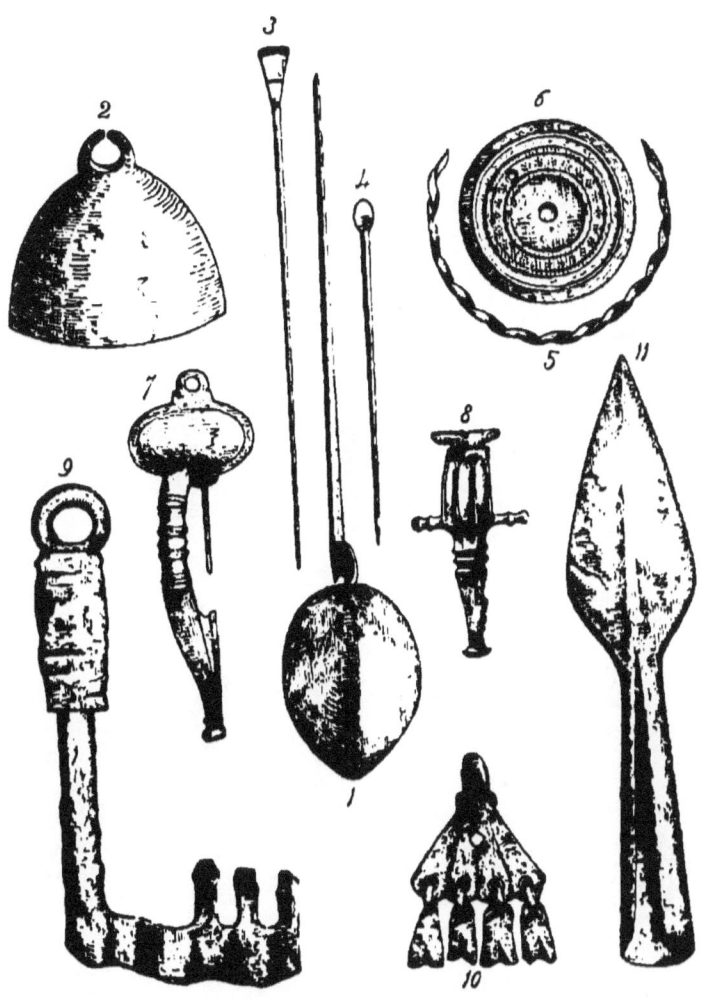

PLATE L.
IMPLEMENTS FOUND ON THE SITE OF THE ROMAN VILLA AT COMBE DOWN.

PLATE LI.
ROMAN CAPITAL FOUND AT WARLEIGH, NEAR BATH.

VILLA AT BOX.—The next Villa that claims attention is situated at Box, about five miles distant from BATH, and on the line of Roman Road leading to Cunetio (Marlborough) and Silchester. The Tessellated Floors of three rooms were found here quite perfect, but the patterns are plain and the work coarsely executed. The most interesting portion is the remains of the Bath, the sides and circular end of which were covered with Tesseræ of white lias. Careful drawings have, I understand, been made of these Pavements, which were situated in gardens in the middle of the village. The remains of a Hypocaust have also been found, with several Pillars entire, and a Roman Bath is also stated to have been found on the south side of the Churchyard.

The Foss Road crosses the top of Banner Down, near the Shire stones, and is not, therefore very far distant from this Villa, which was contiguous to two main Roads.

ROMAN VILLA AT CHENEY COURT.—The Remains of a Roman Villa, and with them several Imperial Coins, were found in July, 1813, near Alcombe, on Cheney Court Farm, south of Road Hill, about five miles from BATH. These are mentioned by Mr. CRANCH, who made a collection of Roman Remains in Walcot, which he catalogued, and afterwards presented to the Corporation of BATH. The Catalogue and Remains are now lodged in the Literary and Scientific Institution.

The Architectural part of the Villa is said to have stood in the orchard at Cheney Court, but little or nothing exists there at the present day.

VILLA AT WARLEIGH.—The Remains of a Villa have been found at Warleigh, near Bathford, about three miles from BATH, on the opposite side of the River Avon. They are described by AUBREY in his Monumenta Britannica.[1] The extract has been kindly sent me by Mr. SKRINE, the possessor of Warleigh Manor, who has deposited in the Museum of the BATH Literary and Scientific Institution, the Capital of a Column, of very elegant workmanship, found on the site of the Villa.[2]

AUBREY states that—

"At Bathford (near the Citie of BATHE) was found, by digging of a draining trench deeper than ordinarily, in the grounds of one Mr. SKRINE, in May, 1655, a room underground, which was about 14 feet one way and 17 feet the other. The Pavement whereof was 'opus tessellatum' of small stones of several colours, viz., white (hard chalk), blue (lias), and red (fire brick). I had several of them, which I gave to the Repository of the Royal Society. In the middle of the Floor was a blue bird, not well proportioned, and in each of the four angles a twisted knot. This

[1] See vol. ii., p. 73.
[2] See plate II.

ground and the whole Manor did belong to the Abbey of BATHE. Underneath this floor is water. The floor is borne on pillars of stone, about an ell distant the one from the other. On the pillars were laid plank stones, on which the 'opus tessellatum' was laid. The water issueth out of the earth a little below, and many pervade themselves there is much water in it.

"This discovered place was so much frequented, that it caused Mr. SKRINE to cover it up again, because the concourse of people, especially from BATHE, damaged his ground; but he would not cover it so soon, but the people had torn up almost all the work before I came hither to see it, but his daughter-in-law hath described the whole floor with her needle in . . . . stitch. Mr. SKRINE told me that there is such another floor adjoining untouched."

ROMAN VILLA AT HASILBURY FARM.—Dr. MUSGRAVE, in his Belgium Britannicum,[1] speaks also of a Tessellated Pavement found at Bathford a short time before he wrote; and he says also that at Hasilbury Farm, 6 miles from BATH, between Box and Corsham, was found in 1710 or 1711 a Villa, 184 feet long, having a Tessellated Pavement.

ROMAN VILLA NEAR IFORD.—If we follow the course of the Valley of the Avon till we come to Freshford, and then take the Valley of the Frome, which will lead us to Farley Castle, we come upon the site of another Roman Villa, situated in Temple Field, half a mile north of Farley towards Iford. The remains were opened in 1822, and a tolerably perfect Roman Bath, several Coins, and some Tessellated Pavement were found. The remains were closed up again.

ROMAN VILLA, FARLEY CASTLE.—There was another Villa about half a mile S. E. from Farley Castle, overlooking Stowford, and on a hill which rises N. W. above it, now occupied by Farley Lodge Farm, are some portions of an Earthwork and Camp.[2] The following account is from a journal of the date Sept. 24, 1822 :—

"The remains of an ancient Roman Villa, with a beautifully Tessellated Pavement, have recently been discovered between Farley Castle and Iford. Indeed the remains have been known to be in existence for a considerable time by persons in the neighbourhood;[3] but for many years they have lain unmolested. Several small Coins have been found, bearing the name of 'TETRICUS,' together with some other curiosities, which are now in the possession of the Rev. Mr. RICHARDSON, the Rector of Farley."

ROMAN VILLA AT COLERNE, WILTS.—In the parish of Colerne, six miles from BATH, on the line of the Foss Way, and almost half a mile to the east of it, the remains of a

[1] Vol I., p. 151.
[2] See the Rev. Canon Jackson's Guide to Farley Hungerford.
[3] A record is given in a History of Somersetshire of some Pavement of the above description having been sent from this place to the Museum at Oxford as far back as the year 1669.

Roman Villa have been discovered. In 1838 some remains were detected while the field was being ploughed, and the occupier of the land caused the spot to be uncovered. It was, however, shortly closed up again, without any drawing or plan being made of the remains laid open. In October, 1851, Mr. EDWARD W. GODWIN, in conjunction with the Vicar, the Rev. GILBERT HEATHCOTE, obtained permission to renew the investigation. The results of their excavations, together with the ground plan, are given in the Arch. Journal.[1]

By their endeavours 11 chambers and two Hypocausts, besides the remains of the foundations of buildings contiguous were laid open, and the drain of the Villa was traced to its outlet. The Pavement originally discovered had been destroyed, and nothing remained but the border of the pattern. According to the description by persons who saw it when uncovered it appears to have had a Chariot in the centre, with a Charioteer and four Horses abreast, and the word SERVIUS or SEVERUS.

The form of the whole building was an oblong running nearly E. and W., with a projecting portion running N. and S., and terminating in an Apse; beyond this again, at the western end, was the Hypocaust. The furnace chamber was constructed of large stones, which from the action of the fire had very much the appearance of very large blue pebbles: the communication between it and the Hypocaust had its sides constructed of bricks an inch thick, while the top and bottom of the aperture were of hard stone.

" In excavating the Hypocaust," says Mr. GODWIN, " no Tesserae were found, although the circular ends were plastered with the same kind of Cement used in the Bath of the Villa at Box, where it was imbedded with white Tesserae. A similar construction to that at Box was found in the Bath at the extremity of the Hypocausts at Uriconium. The pillars, all of which existed in situ, were constructed of hard red stone, in slabs about an inch thick and varying from 10 to 12 inches square. The floor of the Bath Room was one or two steps below the passage pavement. In the passage leading to it, and in the small room in connection with it, another Tessellated Pavement was discovered. This seemed to have been the Dressing Room, with small recesses for attendants adjoining it."

Many Coins were found beyond the portion laid open, and Mr. GODWIN observes that there is little doubt that more extensive remains might be discovered, for several vestiges of masonry have been brought to light by the plough since the date of the excavations described.

ROMAN VILLA AT NORTH WRAXALL.—Since the Remains at Colerne were laid open, another Villa also on the line of the Foss Road, has been completely uncovered, and an accurate plan of it with a description, is given by POULETT SCROPE, Esq., M.P., in the Wilts Arch. and N. H. Mag.[2] It is situated at North Wraxall, and had long been known by

[1] Vol. xiii., p. 328.
[2] Vol. vii., Oct. 1860.

the residents in the neighbourhood as the site of a Roman Station or Villa. A Stone Coffin or Sarcophagus had formerly been dug up there. The field in which the Villa is situated extends over an area of about 3 acres, and forms the brow of a steep wooded slope adjacent to the parish of Castle Combe, which lies to the north of it.

This Villa, like that of Colerne, was an oblong building, measuring about 180 feet by 36 feet, and containing some 16 or more different rooms or enclosures. Of these Mr. SCROPE has given an account, plans, and drawings, as well as a plan of the enclosure in which the Villa was situated, and ground plans of the Out-buildings, marking also the places where Interments were found.

Mr. SCROPE observes that—

"The five small rooms which occupy the western extremity of the range of buildings are its most interesting portion. They all possessed Hypocausts or hot air flues beneath their floors, and together formed a suite of hot bath rooms or thermae. The rooms at the other, or east end, were not provided with any such apparatus, although, from the superior character of the masonry, and the remains of Tessellated Pavements found in them, they would seem to have been some of the principal chambers of the house. The intermediate part of the building was composed of a long corridor on the south side, and on the north side of a series of rooms of different sizes. The walls of the whole building are of good masonry, formed of the oolitic limestone dug on the spot, for the most part well squared and faced with the chisel. They are from 2 feet to 3 feet in thickness."

For particulars I must refer to Mr. SCROPE's interesting paper. The walls of the Bath room as well as those of the other apartments, seem to have been lined with stucco, coarsely painted in various colours, chiefly blue, red, and yellow, in straight stripes or trellis patterns. The number of the Tessellae found in the rubbish shewed that the chambers at the eastern end had once possessed Tessellated Pavements, although of a coarse description. No portion of them remained entire. The rude walling-up of the door ways in some of these rooms seemed to indicate that they had been subjected to alteration. In one of these rooms, a narrow recess, measuring 3 feet in depth by 11 inches in width, was found, and in this, which may have been a sort of cupboard, were discovered the only two entire articles of fragile materials met with in the course of the excavation, viz., an earthenware lipped bowl, lined with silicious grains, called a Mortaria ; and a glass Funnel, which is engraved in the plates accompanying Mr. SCROPE's Paper, and has been rarely met with. One of the most interesting features of this Villa is the Well, which is situated 10 yards from the outer wall of the building just described, the form being externally hexagonal, and internally circular; and measuring 10 feet from angle to angle. On opening out the centre, at the depth of 4 feet the circular shaft was laid bare, and found to be constructed of excellent masonry, every stone being cut to the curve of the circle, which was 3 feet 8 inches in diameter ; the upper courses of the shaft had been removed, and the

ROMAN VILLAS. 123

Well itself filled with rubbish from the adjoining buildings. On being explored, human bones were found, at the depth of 25 feet, and two more Skeletons at the depth of 40 feet. Below this were large fragments of masonry, comprising broken shafts of Columns, with capitals and bases. These latter had been turned in a lathe, and are remarkable for the number of mouldings. Some Pinnacles, like that found at Wellow, were discovered, which had surmounted the ridge of the gables. Their style, as well as that of the Columns, is of the debased character of the Lower Empire. The diameter of the Columns varied from 8 to 12 inches, and as fragments of separate capitals to the number of twelve or more were found, it would appear, says Mr. Schope, that the adjoining buildings had displayed a considerable amount of architectural decoration. Several Coins of the Lower Empire were discovered down the Well shaft. At the depth of 68 feet water appeared.

The building and Well above described were situated within a walled enclosure, measuring 220 ft. by 155 ft., which may have been a garden or court, and in the middle of the south wall were found the square foundations of what were probably the piers of the entrance gates.

Outside of this the foundations of two other separate ranges of buildings were laid bare, each containing several divisions, and the whole enclosed by other boundary walls to the south and east. To the northern extremity of one of these ranges of building there was attached a furnace with its ash-pit, having holes on either side of the masonry, as if to receive iron bars for the support of the fuel.

Squared stones formed of calcareous tuff, full of cavities, were found everywhere among the rubbish, which had been obtained from the side of a neighbouring hill, where it is still deposited in great abundance by a spring strongly impregnated with carbonate of lime. Mr. Schope observes that this stone was probably employed for the vaulting of roofs, owing to its lightness, as a very similar tuff is found so employed by the old Roman builders in many parts of Italy.

The buildings of this Villa had been roofed with Stone-tiles from the Schistose Sandstone of the coal formation of the Vale of the Severn. These were cut into the form of elongated hexagons. The Iron Nails by which the tiles were fastened to the Rafters generally remained. Very strong Timbers must have been required to carry such a roof, as the tiles averaged in weight at least 5 lbs., and measured about 1 foot in width and 18 inches in length.

At the distance of 60 yards outside the western boundary of the group of buildings where the forge was discovered, were the foundations of four or five contiguous chambers measuring inside about 12 feet by 7; the outer walls of the neighbouring chambers being separated by a narrow interval from 18 inches to 2 feet wide. These were found to be places of Sepulture, and Skeletons were discovered, viz.: two bodies buried at full length within Stone Sarcophagi fitted with heavy covers, the Skeletons lying north and south; and two buried at full length, lying east and west, in graves dug 5 feet deep in the rock: one of these was enclosed in a Wooden Coffin; the other in a sort of Cist of separate upright slabs of Stone. A third mode of interment was the ashes of the body inclosed in a Cinerary Urn, within a cavity excavated in a massive Stone.

Each of these several Interments was separately inclosed in a Walled Chamber, The foundation walls of which were not parallel to each other, but had apparently been built at different times; but all appear to belong to the Roman period.

In the course of the excavations many fictile fragments were found. The black, blue, and brown Pottery predominated, but there were also specimens of Durobrivian, and many of Samian ware. A few were of superior quality, and embossed with elegant patterns; one large fragment of a saucer showed the rivet holes by which it had been repaired. Many fragments of glass vessels, and what appeared to have been window glass, were also found. From 24 to 30 Coins were met with in the course of uncovering the buildings: of these, one was a bronze medal of TRAJAN; there were also 2 Coins of ALLECTUS, 1 of MAXENTIUS, some of TACITUS and GRATIANUS, and many of CONSTANTINE. Among other discoveries were two small elegant bronze fibulæ, several bronze rings, two spoons, two or three styli, several ivory hair pins, a large iron key, chisels, knives, cramps, large headed nails, and other iron instruments; a few thin pieces of marble, several of heavy spar, and some polished pebbles apparently used for grinding; bones of cattle, swine, and deer; many oyster shells; many boars tusks, and one very large pair united into an elegant crescent-shaped ornament by means of a bronze sheath, upon which were figures of animals in relief. This, which seems to have been a piece of horse-trapping, was probably hung by a cord round the neck, and formed a pendant for the breast. Such ornaments appear in the sculptures in the column of TRAJAN, and were alluded to in the classic writers.

> ". . . rutiloque monilia torque
> Extrema cervice nitent, ubi pendulus apri
> Deus sedet, et nivea distinguit pectora luna.'

Also—

> ". . . nemorisque notæ sub pectore primo
> Jactantur niveo lunata monilia dente.'"

¹ See Calpurnius Siculus. Ecloga., v. 1., 43.
² Statius, book ix., p. 606.

ROMAN VILLAS.   125

The Villa is distant one mile from the Foss Road, a mile north-east of the Parish Church of North Wraxhall, and about the same distance from Castle Combe. The good state of preservation in which the remains were found is owing to the site having been overgrown with brushwood, which has only been grubbed within the memory of living men, after remaining there ever since the date of the original destruction of the edifice.

It remains only now to mention the sites of a few other Villas, the traces of which are less distinct, and the remains much scantier than those already described.

VILLA AT LANGRIDGE.—The Romans, when in possession of BATH, seems to have been well aware of the advantages of the air of Lansdown, and the beauty of the situation. On the declivity where now stands the parsonage of Langridge, some remains of a Villa have been discovered, and a Stone Coffin, which contained a Skeleton, was disinterred about eight years since: previously to that another had been found, in which were a Skeleton and a "Martel de Fer," the Coffin, as was not unusual, having been used for a second sepulture in the middle ages.

VILLA AT CONGROVE, ON BEACH FARM.—At Congrove, or Coney Grove, on Beach Farm, remains of a Villa have also been discovered; also Querns, Pottery, Coins, Fibulæ, and a Ring. At Coffin Tining, in a field called Uxton Field, north of Upton, on the Road leading to Wick, several Stone Coffins were found. In a field nearer Beach, north-east of Grammers' Rocks, I am informed Remains of a Villa have been traced, and Roman Pottery and a Fibula dug up.

At Farmers' Field, on the opposite side of the Road to Tracey Park, a Villa was laid open some years since. One small Room was uncovered and the floor exposed; many Coins, much Pottery, Bricks, Tiles of stone and brick, a Fibula, pieces of Bone and of Bronze were found, and the field is even now strewed with fragments of Pottery and Roman Brick.

At Hanham Green, 3 miles beyond Bitton, the ancient Abone, on the line of the Via Julia,[1] a Villa seems to have existed, since Roman Pottery and Tiles were found in sinking a well in an Orchard on Mr. WHITTUCK'S Farm. Along the same line of Roman Road, from AQUÆ SOLIS to the Trajectus, about half a mile from Bitton, a Bath was lately discovered, composed of large Slabs of the Lias Rock, which is abundant in that neighbourhood. The sides of these slabs of stone were made to fit tightly into one another by means of hollows

[1] The former Vicar of Bitton, the Rev H E Ellacombe, informs me that this Road is now called by the old people "Aggrin Way," and that he has seen it laid down in an old map as "Augus Way."

or groves in the one, and a corresponding projecting rib in that adjoining, so that by the aid of mortar the Bath was rendered perfectly water-tight. No traces of a Villa, however, have yet been found near where the Bath was discovered in 1862.

Traces of a Roman Villa have been found, and Roman Pottery turned up, on Ash Farm, at North Stoke, between the Church and Village. On Lansdown, near the Road leading from Upton to BATH, towards the western end of the Down, traces of a Roman Building are also stated to have been met with.

Adjoining the same road, and nearer Upton, on the north side, remains of a Villa were explored, and a Ring, Fibula, Coins, Millstone, with numerous pieces of Glass and Pottery were brought to light. The sites of these Villas I have for the most part myself examined; but there are some few localities of which I have been obliged to insert accounts from information given me by persons resident in the neighbourhood, to whose readiness in assisting me I am greatly indebted.

ROMAN VILLA AT BURNETT, IN CORSTON PARISH.—A Roman Villa existed at Corston, three miles west from BATH. The remains are stated to have been laid open more than 30 years ago, when the portions worth preservation were carried to Bristol. A Tessellated Pavement and several small Chambers appear to have been uncovered. Two copper Coins of the Emperor TETRICUS have been found, the one on the site of the Villa and the other in an adjoining field. A quantity of Roman Pottery and Tiles are scattered over the site of the Villa, which was in a field about half way between Burnett and Marksbury, on the south side of the road. No sepulchral remains appear to have been found here, but in a field at Farmborough a Stone Coffin was discovered : this was first used as a trough by the farmer on whose land it was found, and has since been destroyed. For these particulars I am indebted to the courtesy of the present Vicar of Corston.

The remains of several Roman buildings of different sizes have been found along the line of the Foss Road at Camerton. These, which have been described in a paper in the Somerset Archæological and Natural History Society's Journal (1863), appear to have been of small dimensions, but one contained some interesting remains, together with part of an Inscription which fixes the date. The Villa was probably much inferior in size to those already described. There was apparently also a posting Station,— the distance being about seven miles out of AQUÆ SOLIS,—the buildings being contiguous to the line of Roman way. Details are given in the Journal to which I have referred.

ROMAN VILLAS.   127

We have therefore no less than 17 or 18 Villas within a circuit of 7 or 8 miles of BATH, the remains of which have come down to our time, and it is not improbable that others have existed, or that some remains may lie as yet unnoticed. This gives us some idea of the population of the country, and the state of civilization in the Roman period.

There are certain particulars in these Villas which are worthy of notice.

1. The regularity of their form. They were either built round a Court, and formed three sides of a square; or else ran in a straight line, often with a projecting portion at right angles to the main body of the building. They were all provided with a Hypocaust and Baths, and had Tessellated Pavements of elegant workmanship. They were accompanied with out-buildings, and situated in an area of some extent enclosed by a boundary wall, within which were interments of two kinds, viz., cremation and inhumation. The Villas were supplied with earthenware utensils of every description, and with glass, both for windows and domestic use. Coins are found in the greatest abundance, and to the latest period of the Roman occupation. The situations are well chosen, and the Villas are for the most part represented at the present day by elegant modern country houses in the same localities and near the same sites. They were always well supplied with water, and the Wells were of excellent construction.

The Villas around BATH do not seem to have equalled in dimensions those laid open in other parts of England, as at Woodchester or Bignor, nor the elegant remains which exist at Lydney, in Gloucestershire, the plan of which shews something of the luxury and art described in PLINY's account of his Laurentine Villa. It is to be regretted that an account of the remains found at Lydney has never been published, though accurate drawings have been made of them, and all the articles discovered there are carefully preserved by the owner of the property, who exhibited them at the meeting of the Archæological Institute at Gloucester, A.D. 1860.

Mr. WRIGHT, in a very interesting chapter of his "Celt, Roman, and Saxon," has given a sketch of the number of Villas that must have met the eye of the traveller as he journeyed along the line of some of the Roman Roads, but his enumeration of those in Somerset is very limited and imperfect.

The superstructure of these Villas is a subject which has caused much perplexity; and antiquaries are not decided as to whether the upper portions were constructed of stone or wood. I am inclined to think that wood must have furnished the materials of the upper portions, and that the stone walls were only carried to a certain height above the ground floors. The remains seem to indicate that they were hastily plundered and then set fire to, and that the roofs and timbers fell in upon the floors, which are often found indented and covered with burnt matter and roofing tiles. After remaining in this condition, it may be, for centuries, the portions of the walls still standing were afterwards used as quarries, when stone was needed for other buildings or to make enclosures. The Saxon population left them in ruins; the Norman and Mediæval inhabitants used them as materials; and thus little is left to our time except the foundations, and that which lies buried under their débris.

ROMAN CAMPS AND EARTHWORKS AROUND BATH.

THERE are remains of many Earthworks on the hills around BATH and in the immediate neighbourhood. The line of the Wansdyke, coming from the woodlands of Berkshire and passing through Wiltshire into Somerset, may be traced within two miles of the City, on the south side, as it passes over Hampton Down, and is clearly marked at the back of Prior Park. Wansdyke, however, is not Roman, and is only noticed in passing. This interesting Earthwork probably terminated at the Bristol Channel, or at the Camps opposite Clifton, though it cannot be traced further than Macsknoll.[1] There are several Camps along its line as it approaches and leaves BATH, keeping to the south of the City. On Hampton Down there is a fortified British settlement, and near it are traces of a ROMAN CAMP, part of which has been destroyed within the memory of the present generation. It is situated not far from the stone quarries on the top of Bathwick Hill, near to some fir trees, but the use of the plough is fast erasing its distinctive features.. At Stantonbury, distant from BATH about five miles, there is a strong Earthwork, but apparently not of Roman construction ; and at Macsknoll is another, also on the line of Wansdyke, nearer to Bristol. Beyond this point Wansdyke cannot be traced satisfactorily westward,[2] though it is probable the termination was at the two Camps directly opposite Clifton, called Bowre Walls and Stokesleigh, or at Portishead.[3]

North of the Avon, is the isolated hill called Solsbury or Solisbury,[4] the top of which is encircled by an earthen rampart. The strong position of this Camp would lead us to think that it must have been occupied by the Romans. The Earthwork follows the form of the hill, and we know that this arrangement was sometimes adopted by Roman Engineers. The Saxons, also, when they besieged BATH, A.D. 577, probably occupied this position.

[1] For a particular account see Sir R. C. Hoare's Ancient Wilts ; Collinson's Somerset ; the Archæol. Journal, vol. viii., p. 151 (1851); Som. Arch. and Nat. Hist. Soc. Proceedings, vol. vii. (1856).
[2] See Som. Arch. and N. H. Proceedings, vol. vi., p. 111 ; and vol. vii., p. 21. Also, Journal of Brit. Arch. Assoc. (1857), p. 108.
[3] See Journ. Brit. Arch., Assn., 1857, pp. 107 and 108.
[4] See Phelps' Somerset, vol. i., p. 102 ; Collinson, vol. 1, p. 99.

There are two Camps on LANSDOWN undoubtedly of Roman construction. The first of these has been cut through by the Turnpike Road, which passes over Lansdown, within a short distance of Sir BEVILLE GRENVILLE's monument; the other is situated on the western side of the Down, within a few paces of a large Earthwork, apparently of British construction, which cuts off the extremity of the hill. The form of the latter ROMAN CAMP is quite perfect, though the bank and ditch are neither high nor deep.

From the extreme point of the Down where the British Camp is situated, the course of the VIA JULIA may be traced to BITTON, where are the remains of the Roman Station of ABONE, distant about 6 miles.

A Camp[1] is stated to have existed on the hill above Cottage Crescent, and was known by the name of Berewyke, or Berwick Camp; very faint traces of this are now discoverable, as the quarrying of stone has almost effaced any mark of a bank or ditch. Some portions of the hill, however, seem to indicate the course of a rampart, and the spot is well suited for a Camp. COLLINSON mentions that the hill is called the *Barracks*.[2]

A Camp is also said to have existed in Walcot, and also one on the west side of the Avon, at Bathford, but there are no sufficient traces left to make these points certain.

[1] Phelps' Somerset, vol. I, p. 168.
[2] See vol. i., p. 171

ROMAN COINS FOUND IN BATH AND IN THE NEIGHBOURHOOD.

ROMAN Coins in great variety have been found in BATH at different times, but only very small and imperfect collections of them have been made; one belongs to the Corporation, and is lodged in the Literary and Scientific Institution.

Of these Coins the earliest is one of CLAUDIUS, and the latest one of the Emperor GRATIAN, but the earliest Coin found in BATH is one of AUGUSTUS, found at Messrs. SAINSBURY's Brewery.[1] I have been favoured with the following accurate list of the Coins belonging to the Corporation:—

1 Claudius...	...	... 2nd Brass	1 Postumus	...	... 1st Brass
3 Nero ...	..	... 1st „	3 Victorines	...	... 3rd „
1 Galba ...	...	... 2nd „	3 Claudius Gothicus...	... 3rd „
3 Vespasian	...	... 2nd „	1 Diocletian	...	... 2nd „
3 Domitian	...	... 2nd „	3 Maximianus Herculeus	... 2nd „
2 Trajan ...	...	... 1st „	2 Constantinus Magnus	... 2nd „
4 Ditto ...	...	... 2nd „	1 Constantius II.	...	... 3rd „
2 Hadrian ...	...	... 1st „	1 Constans ...	...	... 3rd „
4 Ditto ...	...	... 2nd „	1 Magnentius	...	... 3rd „
6 Antoninus Pius	...	... 1st „	1 Valentinian	...	... 3rd „
4 Ditto ...	...	... 2nd „	4 Valens ...	...	... 3rd „
1 Marcus Aurelius	...	... 2nd „	4 Gratian ...	...	... 3rd „
1 Ditto (Silver)	...	...			
1 Faustina ...	...	... 1st „	64		
1 Commodus	...	... 2nd „	14 Doubtful		
1 Philippus (Billon)	...	...			
1 Gallienus	...	... 3rd „	78 Total		

[1] See next page.

Dr. GUIDOTT, in his Discourse of BATH,[1] gives a list and Drawings of the principal Coins that had been found in his time :—

Brass Coin.
Date A.D. 71.
Obv: IMP CAES VESPASIAN. P. F. AVG., Head of Emperor Wreathed.
R: AEQVITAS AVGVSTI, Female Figure holding a Balance in the Right Hand and a Spear in the left and S. C. on each side of it.

Silver Coin.
Date A.D. 101.
Obv: IMP. TRAJANO. AVG. GER. DAC. P. M. TR. P., Head of Emperor Wreathed.
R: COS. V. P. P. S. P. Q. R. OPTIMO. PRINC., Female Figure with a Balance in the right hand and Cornucopia in the left.

Brass „
A.D. 285.
Obv: IMP. C. CARAVSIVS. P. F. AVG., Head of Emperor Crowned.
R: Female Figure Crowned, holding a Spear in the left hand and a Thunderbolt in the right, on each side B.E. (Britannicus Exercitus). In the Exergue MLXX.

Brass „
A.D. 316.
Obv: CONSTANTINVS. JVN. NOB. C., Head of Emperor encircled by a Wreath.
R: PROVIDENTIAE CAESS, a Palace and a Star above it. Exergue P. TRE.

Brass „
A.D. 224.
Obv: IMP. C. M. AVR. SEV. ALEXAND. AVG., Head of Emperor Wreathed.
R: P. M. T R P. II. COS. P P., Female Figure Seated and Feeding a Serpent out of a Patera.

Silver „
(Found in Glasses.)
A.D. 337.
Obv: D. N. CONSTANTIVS. P. F. AVG., Head of Emperor encircled by a Fillet.
R: A Wreath, and within it VOTIS. XXX. MVLTIS. XXXX. Exergue. P. CON.

Brass „
A.D. 375.
Obv: D. N. VALENTINIANVS. P. F. AVG., Head of Emperor encircled with a Fillet.
R: Victory holding a Palm Branch in the left hand and offering a Garland with the right. SECVRITAS REIPVBLICAE. Exergue. P. CON.

Brass „
(Found at Kelston.)
A.D. 307.
Obv: CONSTANTINO CAES, Head of Emperor Galeated.
R: Victory with Spear and Shield. No legend. Exergue P. TRE.

"These," says Dr. GUIDOTT, " are all the Coins I have met with yet of any value among many others of none at all."

Since Dr. GUIDOTT wrote many more Roman Coins have been discovered. In 1824 some were found when a house near the East Gate was pulled down ; and in 1829, others were found in Bathwick, which are now in the possession of Mr. GOODRIDGE. In removing the foundations of the Old Abbey House, and preparing the site of the present Poor Law Union Board Offices, Coins mostly of the reign of CONSTANTINE the Great, were discovered.

The following is a list of Coins found at Messrs. SAINSBURY's Brewery, BATH, in May, 1815, together with two Stone Coffins, containing Skeletons : either the Coin of CLAUDIUS or that of VESPASIAN was found in one of the Coffins :—

Obv: CAESAR AVGVSTVS. DIVI. F. PATER PATRIAE.
R: An Altar.

Obv: TI. CLAVDIVS. CAESAR.
R: Uncertain.

Obv: IMP. NERO. CAESAR AVG P. MAX. TR.P. P P.
R: VICTORIA. AVGVSTI. S. C.

Obv: NERO CAESAR. AVG. P. MAX.
R: S. C. Victory holding a Shield, on which S.P.Q.N.

[1] Chapter x. p. 66.

ROMAN COINS. 133

Obv: IMP. CAESAR. VESPASIAN. AVG. COS. III.
R. PAX. AVG. S. C. Female holding Patera.
The same, so much corroded as to be illegible.
Obv: IMP. CAES. DOMIT. AVG. GERM. COS. XIII.
R: FORTVNAE. AVGVSTI. S. C.
Obv: IMP. CAES. DOMIT. AVG. GERM. COS. XIII CENS. PER. P. P
R. MONETA. AVGVSTI. S. C.
Obv: IMP. CARAVSIVS. P. F. AVG.
R. PAX. AVG. S. C.
Obv: CONSTANTINVS. MAX. AVG.
R. GLORIA. EXERCITVS.

The above Coins are 2nd Brass, with the exception of the two last, which are 3rd Brass.

A Coin of AUGUSTUS, found at Wellow, was in the possession of the late Rev. C. PAUL.

A Gold Coin of NERO is stated to have been discovered A.D. 1857, in making a sewer.

A Coin of CARAUSIUS, 3rd brass, said to have been found in BATH, was purchased for the British Museum, and is recorded and engraved in the proceedings of the Archæological Institute.[1]

Obv: Head of Emperor.
R. A Trophy of Arms, with two Captives at its feet, Legend VICT. GERM.

When the Cemetery in Lyncombe Vale was formed A.D 1843, the following Coins were discovered with an interment, and were deposited near the Coffin. CONSTANTINE (3 Coins), CARAUSIUS, GALLIENUS, and two doubtful, all brass.

At the ascent of Bathwick Hill, A.D. 1819, near the Coal Wharf (which was then being formed), a Box containing 8 small Roman Coins, all of the Lower Empire, was discovered near some interments; also Copper Coins of Vespasian were found with an interment in Russell Street, A.D. 1818 ; and in 1852 further interments with the following Coins in the Earth around the Coffins :—

Brass. 1. *Obv*: GRATIANUS, Head of Emperor.
 R. Warrior, with Prostrate Figure; R. C. on each side.
 Legend: EXERCITVS.

Silver Coin of 2. *Obv*: IMP. ANTONIN. PIVS. AVG.
Heliogabalus. *R*. Figure standing before an Altar, with a Patera in the right hand, over which is a Star.
 Legend: PM. TR. P. V. COS. IIII. P. P.

Brass 3. *Obv*: CONSTANTINVS. IVN. NOB. C.
 R. Two Figures with a Standard between them.
 Legend: Effaced.

4. *Obv*: CONSTANTINVS. AVG.
 R. Cuppa, with Globe on it; above Globe Three Stars (on the Cyppus, VOTIS. XX.)
 Legend: BEATA TRANQUILLITAS.
 Exergue: P. T M.

[1] Vol. ix., p. 194.

The following is a list of the Coins found when the Site of the New Building added to the Mineral Water Hospital was cleared A.D. 1859 :—

Trajan	...	...	2	Valentinian	...	...	2	Copper 2
Hadrian	...	...	1	Valens	...	...	4	Pop: Rom; 1
Gallienus	...	...	2	Arcadius	...	...	1	Julia Paula (?) 1
Victorinus	...	...	4	Albinus (?)	...	...	1	Maximus 1
Tetricus	...	...	4	Valerianus	...	...	1	Urbs Roma 1
Aurelian	...	...	1	Valentinus	...	...	1	Illegible 43
Constantine	...	...	4	Claudius Gothicus	...	1		
Carausius	...	...	7	Byzantium	...	...	1	
Constantine	...	...	5	Geta	...	...	1	
Constantine, Junior	...	2	Gratian (Silver)	...	1		Total 95

The Coins extend over a period of from A.D. 98 to A.D. 408.

The above statement is given only to shew how plentiful have been the Roman Coins found in BATH. It would be impossible to obtain a correct list of all that have been discovered. The neighbourhood of BATH has been equally productive, as will appear by the two following lists of Coins found at Combe Down and at Bitton, both within a very short distance of the City. The author is indebted to J. RETTINGTON, Esq., of Bathwick Hill, for the lists of those found at Messrs. SAINSBURY'S Brewery and Combe Down; and to the Rev. H. T. ELLACOMBE, M.A., Rector of Clyst St. George, for the list of Coins found at Bitton, of which parish he was formerly Vicar.

Roman Coins found in Mr. CRUIKSHANK's Garden at Combe Down :—

2nd and 3rd *Brass*, very much corroded, but evidently of the Constantine period — 151

Denarii—a Broken Coin *of Septimius Severus*,—REVERSE. PIVS. AVG., Laureated Head, R/. PART. MAX. P.
  M. TR. P. E.—Trophy of Arms, at foot two Captives 1

IMP. SEV. ALEXAND. AVG., Laureated Head, R/. F. M. TR. P. COS. II. P. P.—The Emperor Marching, carrying Spear and Trophy 1

D. N. CONSTANTIVS. P. F. AVG., Diadem'd Head, R/. VOTIS. XXX. MVLTIS. XXXX., in a Crown of Laurel—
  Exergue P. CON. 1

D. N. VALENS. P. F. AVG., Laureated Head, R/. RESTITVTOR. R E i P.—The Emperor holding the Labarum and a Globe, surmounted with a Victory. Exergue P. LVG. 1

Large Brass.
IMP. SEV. ALEXANDER. AVG., Laureated Head, R/. VIRTVS. AVGVSTI. S.C. 1

2nd Brass.
ANTONIA—Wife of Nero Drusus. ... ...
DOMITIAN—R. MONETA AVGVSTI. S.C. 3
FAVSTINA. SEN. ... ...

2nd and 3rd Brass.
CLAVDIVS GOTHICVS.	...	...	...	...	...	...	...	...	2
TETRICVS. SEN.	...	...	...	...	...	...	...	...	5
TETRICVS. JUN.	...	...	...	...	...	...	...	...	1
CARAVSIVS.	...	...	...	...	...	...	...	...	3
HELENA—Mother of Constantine	...	...	...	...	...	...	...	2
CONSTANTINE (the Great)	...	...	...	...	...	...	...	14
VRBS. ROMA—4. CONSTANTINOPOLIS—7									11
CONSTANTINE. JVN.	...	...	...	...	...	...	...	9
CONSTANS.	...	...	...	...	...	...	...	...	11
CONSTANTIVS. II.	...	...	...	...	...	...	...	...	1
MAGNENTIVS.	...	...	...	...	...	...	...	...	2
VALENTINIAN.	...	...	...	...	...	...	...	...	5
VALENS	...	...	...	...	...	...	...	...	7
GRATIAN	...	...	...	...	...	...	...	...	1

COINS FOUND AT BITTON

Valentinian I., A.D. 364.

No. 1.   D. N. VALENTINIANVS. P F. AVG.
         Head of the Emperor.
         R/. VIRTVS EXERCITVS.   Valentinian standing erect, holding the Labarum and a Globe.   Ex. LVG.

Valentinian II., A.D. 383.

No. 2.   D. N. VALENTINIANVS. IVN. P. F. AVG.
         Head of the Emperor.
         R/. VRBS. ROMA.   Rome seated, holding a Victory and a Hasta.   Ex. AQ. PS.

No. 3.   DITTO.
         R/. VIRTVS. EXERCITVS.   The Emperor holding a Standard and a Globe.

Gratian, A.D. 367.

No. 4.   D. N. GRATIANVS. P. F. AVG.
         Head of the Emperor.
         R/. VIRTVS ROMANORVM.   Rome seated, holding a Globe and the Hasta reversed.   Ex. AQ. PS.

No. 5.   DITTO.
         R/. Ditto.   Ex. TR. PS.

No. 6.   DITTO.
         R/. VOT. X. MVLT. XX in a Laurel Crown.

No. 7.   DITTO.
         R/. VIRTVS ROMANORVM., as No. 4.

No. 8.   DITTO.
         R/. VIRTVS ROMANORVM., as No. 4.

Eugenius, A.D. 392.

No. 9.   D. N. EVGENIVS. P. F. AVG.
         Head of the Emperor to the right.
         R/. VIRTVS ROMANORVM.   Rome seated, holding a Globe, surmounted by a Victory
         All Copper or Billon.
         Silver.

Arcadius, A.D. 395.

No. 10.   D. N. ARCADIVS. P. F. AVG.
         R/. VIRTVS ROMANORVM.   Rome seated.   Ex. M D P S.

No. 11.   CONSTANTIVS.   A.D. 306.

No. 12.   TETRICVS.

No. 13.   Small Coin, found A.D. 1822, in Mrs. Mantell's Garden.

ROMAN REMAINS RECENTLY FOUND IN BATH.

WHILE the earlier sheets of this Volume were passing through the press, discoveries of Roman Remains have been made on the ground cleared for the enlargement of the Bath United Hospital; both on the portion to be occupied by the Albert Wing, and on the site of the Rooms for the Medical Officers. The nature of the building which has stood on the site of the Albert wing, is not yet satisfactorily ascertained. The Remains consist of strong Foundation Walls running east and west, with portion of a Hypocaust; and a room with a circular apse. Bricks, Tesserœ, Flue Tiles, and Pottery have also been found, and burnt matter, together with the base of a Pilaster, no doubt the relic of a former structure, which had been used as old material and inverted and imbedded in the foundation of the building. The level of the Roman floors is about 9 ft. 6 in. below the surface of the present roadway in Beau Street. The construction of the masonry is as follows :—Foundation laid in clay, in which large pebbles are imbedded; upon these a bed of concrete, then a course of tiles, then masonry with joints inclined, somewhat resembling herring-bone, upon which stones are laid in regular courses. Two Baths at different levels have been partially uncovered.

Herring-bone masonry has also been found beyond the apse of the room situated next to the old portion of the Hospital. One of the large stones in the walling has a deep-cut cross upon it like the Greek *tau*. The Hypocaust was towards Westgate Street, at the eastern side of the building. A Coin of the Emperor ANTONINUS PIUS, in good preservation, bearing an Elephant on the reverse, has been found in the course of excavating; also a Tile with the foot-print of a dog upon it.

At the south-east angle of the old Building the floor of a chamber, about 12 feet square, has been discovered, resting upon pilæ of stone or brick, and covered with a Tessellated Pavement, which, though much broken and defaced, reveals traces of very elegant workmanship. In the centre is a geometrical pattern, composed of small Tesserœ, the colours of which are white, blue, red, black, and green, shaded very finely into one another, so as to form a pleasing and harmonious composition.

The Stone[1] found in preparing the foundations of the present Hospital in 1825, indicated the erection of some structure by the SON OF NOVANTUS "pro se et suis," and from the remarkable reason assigned for its erection ("ex visu posuit,") it is open to us to infer that the latter of these structures now laid bare may have been the floor of a small Temple or Sacred Edifice, erected by this devout Heathen.

[1] For description see p. 73 supra.

A careful plan of the part uncovered has been made, but not sufficiently in time for insertion in this volume. It is hoped that the nature of the building may eventually be accurately ascertained.

On preparing the ground for the Foundation of St. John's Church, Bathwick, in 1861, the remains of an ancient drain or flue were discovered; and at the same time portions of a wall, part of a column, and some fragments of Roman pottery. The section of the ground was as follows :—

    1. Loose soil deposited from time to time, 7 feet deep.
    2. Burnt earth and debris, 10 inches deep, in which part of a column[1] was found.
    3. Undisturbed earth resting on gravel.

The Drain or Flue ran under the north-west entrance porch of the nave and was met with again, about midway, in digging the foundation of the north wall of the Church. It was about 11 inches wide and 13 inches deep, the bottom being formed of finely sifted gravel concrete. The direction of the ancient wall which accompanied this flue or drain and ran parallel to it, was N.E. and S.W., and seemed to pass under the chancel. The depth from the level of the floor of the nave to the bottom of the flue was 11 feet 9 inches. Some Roman building, therefore, probably stood near the site of the old Church which was pulled down about A.D. 1818, but no record has been found of any discovery then made or when the present Rectory House was built A.D. 1777.

In digging the foundation for one of the buttresses which support the Dome of the New Market, erected 1863, a stone figure of a Lion was discovered. This is now placed in the Literary and Scientific Institution. Two or three small Roman Coins are said to have been found near it, at a depth which was about the level of the ancient Roman City.

[1] Deposited in the Museum of the Bath Lit. & Sci. Inst.

SUBSCRIBERS.

                                                                COPIES
Antiquaries Society of London ... ...
Archæological Institute of Great Britain and Ireland... 1
Ashlaston Louisa The Lady 1
Algar Miss, Bathwick Hill, Bath 1
Atherley Miss, 27, Pulteney Street, Bath ... 1
Atkinson Mrs., Sydney Place, Bath... 1

Bath the Marquis of, Longleat 1
Broughton The Rt. Hon. Lord, Tidworth ... 1
Bath Corporation 1
Bath Literary and Scientific Institution ... 1
Babington Professor, M.A., F.R.C.S., St. John's College,
  Cambridge 1
Badie Rev. Alexander, Bath 1
Bannatyne Mrs. Chalvedon, Weston Park, Bath ... 1
Bartrum J. S., Esq., Guy Street, Bath ... 1
Barnwell Rev. E. Lowry, M.A., Secretary of the
  Cambrian Archæological Association ... 1
Bissett Mrs. C. H., 15, Bruch Street, Bath ... 1
Birch Peter, Esq., Shrewsbury 1
Bettington John H., Esq., Villa Bianca, Bath ... 1
Bettington Joseph, Esq., Bathwick Hill, Bath ... 1
Birkett Mrs. Crawford, Regent's Park, London ... 1
Blaxland the Hon. John, New South Wales ... 1
Bond Rev. John, Weston Vicarage, near Bath ... 1
Brabazon Dr., Darlington Street, Bath ... 1
Brackstone R. H., Esq., Bath 1
Brakub Mrs. 1, Grosvenor Place, Bath ... 2
Bradford R., Esq., Medge Hall, Wilts ... 1
Brent John, Esq., F.S.A., Canterbury ... 1
Brown Mrs. Edward 1
Bruce Rev. J. Collingwood, D.D., Newcastle-on-Tyne... 1
Brushfield Dr., County Asylum, Chester ... 1
Brymer Mrs., Pulteney Street, Bath ... 1
Burkle Rev. G., Turston, near Bath ... 1
Burrell Joseph, Esq., Lincoln's Inn, London ... 1
Burrell Godfrey, Esq., 3, Darlington Place, Bath ... 1
Bursingham George, Esq., Widcombe Hill House, Bath 1
Burne Dr., Richmond Lodge, Bath 1
Bush W., Esq., Circus, Bath 1
Buttanshaw Rev. John, 25, St James's Square ... 1
Byrom Henry, Esq., Byland House, Bath ... 1

Carnarvon the Right Hon. the Countess Dowager of,
  Pixton Park 1
Cleveland His Grace the Duke of, Raby Castle ... 1
Cleveland Her Grace the Duchess of, ditto ... 2
Cockburn Lady, Doulton Rectory, Devon 1

                                                                COPIES
Caillard C. F. D., Esq., Judge of the County Courts of
  Somersetshire and Wiltshire, Wingfield House ... 1
Clayton John, Esq., Chesters, Hexham, Northumberland 2
Collyns Rev. C. H., Park Street, Bath ... 1
Conolly C. J. T., Esq., Cottles House, Atworth ... 1
Cottrell J. H., Esq., Bewdley Villa, Bath ... 1
Crawley Rev. E. J., The Cedars, Bath ... 1
Cruickshank George, Esq., Helmaud House, Combe
  Down, Bath 1
Cruttwell T., Esq., Bath 1

Devonshire His Grace the Duke of, Devonshire House,
  London, &c. 1
Dynevor the Right Hon. Lord, 19, Prince's Gardens,
  Kensington 1
Davis Sir J. F., Bart., K.C.B., Hollywood, Bristol ... 1
Davis C. E., Esq., F.R.A., 55, Pulteney Street, Bath... 1
Davies Mr. James, Bookseller, Bath 3
De Wilde G. J., Esq., Northampton 1
Doane Rev. J. R., 19, Som Hill, Bath ... 1
Dickenson F. H., Esq., King-Weston House, Somerton... 2
Dillwyn Mrs., I, Raby Place, Bath ... 1
Doham Wm., Esq., Oakwood, Bath 3
Dorman Mark, Esq., Mayor of Northampton... 1
Duveton Rev W. Blake, Corston Vicarage ... 1
Devoward George, Esq., Meols Bruce, Salop ... 1
Drought Miss, Sydney Place, Bath 1
Dryden Rev. Sir H., Canons Ashby ... 1
Duharle M. Achille, Belmont, Bath ... 1
Dunlop D. M., Esq., Kilhenny House, Bath ... 1

Ellenborough the Right Hon. the Earl of, Southam
  House, Cheltenham 1
Earle Rev. J., Swanswick, Bath 1
Earle Rev. A., Monckton Farley 1
Ewart W., Esq., M.P., Broadleas, Devizes ... 1

Franklin Lady 1
Fagan Colonel 1
Fairholt F W., F.S.A., 24, Montpellier Square, Brompton 1
Falconer Thos., Esq., Col. Monmouthshire, Judge of the
  County Courts of Glamorganshire and Brecknockshire
Falconer Randle W., Esq., M.D., 22, Bennett Street Bath 1
Falkner Francis Henry, Esq., Lyncombe Vale, Bath ... 1
Falkner Francis, Esq., Crag Hall, Bath ... 1
Falkner Frederick, Esq., Lyncombe Vale, Bath ... 1
Falkner John Stringer, Esq., Beacon Hill Villa, Bath... 1
Falls Dr., Hampstead House, Bournemouth 1

SUBSCRIBERS.

	copies
Fitzgerald Col., 9, Marlborough Buildings, Bath	1
Florian Felix, Esq., St. James's Street, Bath	1
Frank: Augustus, Esq., Director of the Society of Antiquaries, British Museum	1
Freeman Col., Johnstone Street, Bath	1
George Rev. P. E., Combe Hay, Bath	1
Godwin C., Esq., Norfolk Crescent, Bath	...
Goodford Rev Dr., Provost of Eton College	...
Goodwin J., Esq., F.S A., 12, Edward Street, Bath	1
Gore Arthur, Esq., Melksham	1
Grant John, Esq., The Manor, Manningford Bruce	1
Gray J., Esq., Summerhill House, Bath	1
Grenville Ralph Neville, Esq., Butleigh Court, Glastonbury	...
Gresley Rev J. M., The Lodge, Etwall Hospital, Derby	1
Grove Mrs H. and Miss, Sedwick Hill, Bath	...
Guise W. V., Esq., F.L.S., F.G.S., Elmore Court, Gloucester	1
Hale The Ven. Archdeacon, Charterhouse, London	1
Hale Col. Alderley, Wootton-under-Edge	...
Hall Richard C., Esq., Corston, Bath	2
Hamilton Rev. Leveson E., Alma Villas, Bath	...
Harries C. A., Esq., Walcot Parade, Bath	...
Harwood Major, The Elms, Ringmer, Sussex	2
Hawley Rev. W. Douglas, Isle of Man	1
Hawks Rev. W., Sydney Place, Bath	...
Hayward N., Esq., Express Office, Bath	...
Heathcote Rev. G., Colerne	...
Henney Rev. Dr., Merchant Taylor's School	...
Henney Rev. Dr., Francis, The Parsonage, Kensington, London	1
Henney Rev. Reld. Falkner, Magdalen College, Oxford	1
Hewitt Capt. William Vigors, 3, Church Street, Widcombe, Bath	1
Hill G. D., Esq., Learn Place, Bath	1
Hill Miss, 16, Phillimore Gardens, Kensington, London	1
Hony Lieut.-Col., 9, Eaton Place, London	1
Horner Rev. John S. H., Mells Rectory, Frome	1
Horton Miss, 1s, Brock Street, Bath	1
Hugo Rev. Thos., Pierville, Clapton, London	1
Hunt Kaye, Esq., Bath	...
Hunt Miss. 20, St. James's Square, Bath	...
Hunter Julian, Esq., M.D., Bath	1
Jervis Lady, Bailbrook Lodge, Bath	...
Jackson Rev. Canon, F.S A., Leigh Delamere	1
Jackson Rev. Thos., Sydney Buildings, Bath	1
Jackson Miss, Shrewsbury	...
Jessyns Rev. L., President of Bath Natural History and Antiquarian Field Club, &c., 1, Darlington Place, Bath	1
Jessop Charles Moore, Esq., M.R.C.S., Castle Hill Fort, Dover	1
Johnstone D., Esq., 13, Marlborough Buildings, Bath	1
Jones Rev. W. H., F.S.A., Bradford-on-Avon	1
Jones Col. Inigo, Kelston Park, Bath	1
Kemble Rev. Chas., Rector of Bath, Vellore, Bath	1
Kenrick Rev. John, F.S.A., Monkgate, York	1
Kerslake Mr., Bristol	1
Kilvert Rev. Francis, Executors of the late	2
Lyell Sir Chas., Bt., F S A., President British Association	1
Langton W. H. Gore, Esq., M.P., Newton Park, Bath	1
Lasbury Mr. Olive, Bristol	1
Lean George Binchey, Esq., 3, Cavendish Crescent, Bath	1

	copies
Lee J. E., Esq., Caerleon, Monmouthshire	...
Lewis Mrs., Cornwall Villa, Bathwick Hill, Bath	1
Lewis Mrs., Dennel Hill, Chepstow	...
Ley Rev. Jacob, Staverton Vicarage, Daventry	1
Ley Rev. John, Waldron Rectory, Uckfield	1
Ley Miss, Sowton Rectory, Exeter	...
Little Capt. Alexander, R.N., 70, Pulteney Street, Bath	1
Long W., Esq., 16, Lansdown Place East, Bath	1
Lysons Rev. Samuel, M.A., F.S.A., Hempsted Court, near Gloucester	1
Malahide Lord Talbot de, Malahide Castle, and Evercreech	2
Midleton Very Rev. and Right Hon. Lord Viscount, Dean of Exeter	1
Miles Sir Wm., Bart., M.P., Leigh Court, Bristol	1
Murchison Sir Roderick Impey, F.R.S., F.G.S.	1
March Jerom, Esq., Mayor of Bath, Cranwells, Bath	1
MacDonnell Mrs., Friar Lodge, Lyncombe, Bath	1
Macphail Rev. W. R. Maur, Farringdon Gurney, Wilts	1
Markland J. H., Esq., D.C.L., F.R.S., F S.A., Lansdown Crescent	1
Mathewman Mrs., Alma House, Headington, Leeds	1
Mathew Mrs. Fetton, Locksley, Northam, Devonshire	1
May Mr. F., Bookseller, Taunton	1
M'Caul Rev. John, LL.D., President of the University College, Toronto	1
Meek Mrs., Hillworth House, Devizes	1
Mitchell Mrs., 5, Titchfield Terrace, Regent's Park	1
Mitchell Miss, 4, Raby Place, Bath	...
Mony H. J., Esq., Midsomer Norton	...
Morgan Octavius, Esq., M.P., F.S.A.	...
Morgan John, Esq., 3, Sussex Place, Hyde Park Gardens	1
Mortowe Rev. W. D., Lenebridge Deverill, Warminster	1
Morres Miss Mary, 29, Pulteney Street, Bath	1
Morris Mrs., 14, Pulteney Street, Bath	1
Moss Rev. J. Y., 0, Sion Place, Bath	1
Moore Chas., Esq., F.G.S., Bath	...
Moule Major-General, Belmont, Melksham	...
Moulton Stephen, Esq., Kingston House, Bradford-on-Avon	1
Murchison E. R., Esq., Manor House, Bathford	...
Newnham, Capt., R.N., Dunsford Place, Bath	1
Nichols Rev. W L., Kensham House	1
Nichols Miss, Hanger Hill, near London	1
Nichols John Gough, Esq., F.S.A., &c., Brighton, and Parliament Street, Westminster	1
Northey Lieut.-Col., Clavertoon Manor, Bath	1
Nutt Rev. C. H., Harptree	1
Ormerod Geo., Esq., Sedbury Park, Chepstow	1
Powis the Rt. Hon. the Earl, 45, Berkeley Square, London	1
Palairet Rev. R., Norton St. Philip's	1
Pardin Rev. Canon, Cottles House, Atworth, Wilts	1
Paris Robert, Esq., Ringwood, Hants	...
Payne K. T., Esq., Bath	...
Petit Rev. John L., Esq., 9, New Square, Lincoln's Inn	1
Phelps Mrs., Bathwick Hill, Bath	1
Potts Miss, Watergate Street, Chester	1
Poynder T. H A., Esq., M A., Hartham Park, Bath	1
Pretty Edward, Esq., F.S.A., Chillington House, Maidstone	1
Price Miss, The Grove, Port Hill, Shrewsbury	1
Prideaux George Fisher, Esq., Glenmaire Lodge, Cotham, Bristol	1

SUBSCRIBERS.

Pringle Mrs., Bathwick Hill, Bath — 1
Pycroft Rev. J., 27, Gloucester Gardens, London — 1

Quekett Edward, Esq., Parrett Lodge, Langport — 1
Quan J., Esq., National Provincial Bank, Bath — 1

Rainey Mr James, 6, Widcombe Crescent, Bath — 1
R. J. L. L. — ... — ... — 1
Rathbone R. Reynolds, Esq., St. Michael's Hamlet, near Liverpool — 1
Rawlins C. Wyndham, Esq., 30, Pulteney Street, Bath — 1
Roberts Mr. W., Bookseller, Broadgate, Exeter — 1
Roscoe Mrs., Bathwick Hill, Bath — 1
Rowley Rev. Dr., Willey Rectory, Bridgnorth — 1

Style Sir Charles, Bart., 102, Sydney Place, Bath — 1
Salisbury The Very Rev. the Dean of, Deanery, Salisbury — 1
Salmon Erre, Esq., Holcombe House, Stratton — 1
Sandford W., Esq., 9, Springfield Place, Bath — 1
Saunders T. W., Esq., Recorder of Bath — 1
Sayce Rev. Henry R., Apsley House, Bathampton — 1
Scarth Jonathan, Esq., Shrewsbury — 1
Scarth T. F., Esq., Keverstone, Darlington — 1
Scarth Mrs., Keverstone, Darlington — 1
Scarth W Thos., Esq. — 1
Scholefield W., Esq., M P., Reform Club, London — 1
Scott Mrs., Duke Street, Bath — 2
Shaw Mrs., Beechen Cliff Villa, Bath — 1
Shum Mr. F., Henrietta Street, Bath — 1
Simmons Henry Argent, Esq., Spa Villa, Bathwick Hill, Bath — 1
Simms Miss, Spa Villa, Bathwick Hill, Bath — 1
Simms George H., Esq., Montebello, Bathwick Hill, Bath — 1
Simms Mr. S. W., Bookseller, Bath — 2
Skrine Henry Duncan, Esq., Manor House, Warleigh — 1
Slade Mrs., Pulteney Street, Bath — 1
Smith Hubert, Esq., St. Leonard's, Bridgnorth, Shropshire — 1
Smith Miss Abingdon, 20, Royal Crescent, Bath — 1
Solly Miss, 52, Marlborough Buildings, Bath — 1
Spode J., Esq., Hawkesyard Park, near Rugeley, Staffordshire — 1
Spode Mrs., Hawkesyard Park, near Rugeley, Staffordshire — 1
Steele Rev. Dr., Bathwick Terrace, Bath — 1
Stratton Joseph, Esq., Manningford Bruce, Marlborough, Wilts — 1
Stone John, Esq., Town Clerk of Bath — 1

Stothert, John, Esq., Bathwick Hill, Bath — 1
Stothert Richard, Esq., Raby Place, Bath — 1
Stothert Mrs. Henry, 5, Perrymead, Bath — 1
Symonds Dr., Clifton Hill House, Clifton — 1

Taylor W., Esq., Harptree Court, Bristol — 1
Thomas Henry Harington, Esq., 77, Pulteney Street, Bath — 1
Thompson Mrs., Thingwall Hall, Liverpool — 1
Tite W., Esq., M.P., Lowndes Square, London — 2
Trevor Alfred S., Esq., The Vinery, Bridgnorth — 1
Tucker Charles, Esq., Marlands, Exeter — 1
Tugwell George Clutterbuck, Esq., Crew Hall, Bath — 1
Tugwell Rev. George, Ilfracombe — 1

Uttermore Thos. B., Esq., Langport — 1

Vans the Lord Harry, Battle Abbey — 1
Vaughan John Esq., Raby Villa, Bath — 1
Vivian G. Esq., Claverton Manor, and Upper Grosvenor Street, London — 1

Waldron Mrs., Bathwick Hill, Bath — 1
Walker Thos. F. W., M.A., F.R.G.S., 6, Brock Street, Bath — 1
Wansey W., Esq., Bognor, Sussex, and Reform Club, London — 1
Ware Captain, 1, Pelham Villas, S. Kensington — 1
Warner Rev. J. Lee, Thorpland, Fakenham — 1
Watson Thomas Bunden, Esq., M.D., 9, Lansdown Crescent, Bath — 2
Way Albert, Esq., Wonham Manor, Reigate, Surrey — 1
Wemyss Mrs., 3, Green Park Buildings, Bath — 1
Whittington John, Esq., Queen's Parade Place, Bath — 1
Willett Mrs. G., 11, Lansdown Crescent, Bath — 1
Winwood Rev. Henry H., M.A., 4, Cavendish Crescent, Bath — 1
Wood Rev. James, M.A., 10, Burlington Street, Bath — 1
Woodward R., Esq., Chargrove, Cheltenham — 2
Wollaston Dr., Stafford — 1
Wright William, Esq., Sigglesthorne Hall, near Hull, Yorkshire — 1

Yalden Mrs., Alphington, Exeter — 1
Yeats James, Esq., M.A., F.R.S., Lauderdale House, Highgate — 1
Yates Miss Ellen, Farmfield, near Liverpool — 1

R. E PEACH, PRINTER, BRIDGE STREET, BATH

www.ingramcontent.com/pod-product-compliance
Lightning Source LLC
Chambersburg PA
CBHW031812230426
43669CB00009B/1107